Who Will Be
Left Behind
and When?

Dave Bussard

Strong Tower Publishing

Strong Tower Publishing
P. O. Box 973
Milesburg, PA 16823

ISBN 0-9704330-2-6

Cover design by Wade Thompson

Table of Contents

Table of Charts

Dedication

To my wife, Carmen. Thank you for letting me ignore you all these months while my head was buried in my Bible and my fingers tapped on the keyboard just about every night. With your patience, this book was made possible.

Acknowledgments

Like most who are born into the mainstream of Evangelicalism, I was a pre-tribber from birth. It wasn't until my early twenties that I began studying the scriptures for myself because of my newfound excitement for God and my life-changing encounter with Him. I began studying every prophecy position I could lay my hands on and soon understood their points and reasoning, but that didn't make them fit into what I saw Christ, Paul, John, and others in the scriptures saying about the issue.

A sincere "thank you" to Robert Van Kampen and Marvin Rosenthal for their books on this subject. An extra special "thank you" to Gary Vaterlaus, national instructor for The Sign Ministries (now absorbed into Sola Scriptura Ministries), which was started by Van Kampen after publication of his book *The Sign*. Much of the content of the coming pages I learned directly from these men and their personal devotion to study.

Thank you, H. L. Nigro for your thought-provoking book and belief in this project. Your willingness to go above and beyond with your editing skills is gratefully appreciated. Your correspondences have been very encouraging for, as you know, there are more critics than advocates of our position and it is nice to have an ear.

This book would have had stick-men on the cover if it weren't for Wade Thompson and his graphic design skills. Thank you, Wade.

Thank you, Scott, for listening to me ramble on and on about this subject on our many fishing trips together, even though I know, at times, you were tired of listening. Without you, my wife would have had to hear it all. You're a better and more patient friend than I. Not a better fisherman, though.

And last, but certainly not least, I sincerely thank all the men and women who proofread this book more than once and gave me many criticisms and encouragements. I couldn't have done it without you.

Introduction: Things May Be Different Than You Think

Did you know that there are 8,352 Bible verses related to prophecy?[1] I recently read that Billy Graham has found 380 references to the Second Coming in the scriptures![2] And my wife has informed me that, according to Max Lucado, 23 of the 27 books in the New Testament refer to Christ's return. It must be important!

Here are some other things you might not know about end-times prophecy:

• Did you know that, despite the popularity of the pre-tribulation rapture teaching, there is only one verse (Rev. 3:10) in the entire Bible that even *appears* to say we *might* be raptured before the 70th Week of Daniel (what most call the seven-year Tribulation)?

• Did you know that most people think we will be raptured before Daniel's 70th Week because the Bible says we are not destined for God's wrath, but for salvation; and yet there is not one verse in the Bible that says the entire 70th Week of Daniel is God's wrath? (In fact, there are many passages that say something quite different, therefore setting aside the need for the Church to be raptured pre-tribulationally.)

• And did you know that, while almost all of us believe

---

[1] *Encyclopedia of Biblical Prophecy*, J. Barton Payne, Harper & Row Publishing, 1973, p. 675.

[2] *Before God's Wrath: The Bible's Answer to the Timing of the Rapture*, H. L. Nigro, Strong Tower Publishing, 2000, p. 18.

that the rapture will come like a thief in the night and take us by surprise, Jesus and Paul tell us that it will not surprise the believer, that we will know when the time is near, and that it will surprise only the nonbeliever?

I'm sure you've heard that Christ could come at any moment because nothing has to happen before His return. And yet, there is not one passage that says this! In fact, there are many scriptures that tell us there are certain events that *must* happen first.

I understand that these statements may be difficult to swallow, and at first might sound like false teachings to many, but have patience, a desire for truth, and read ahead to find firsthand that the majority isn't always right.

Who Are You Listening To?

Think about the people of Israel who were living at the time of Christ. Who were they listening to as their spiritual authorities? For many, it was the Pharisees. The Pharisees were the religious leaders of that time, and very few dared to question their authority. The truth had been deformed to the point that it had become so complicated that many just relied on the leaders for answers.

Many great people at that time had scriptural assumptions and expected the Messiah to come in a certain way at His First Coming. They "knew" He would come as a government ruler, world leader, and earthly king. When Jesus came as a carpenter, humble servant, and final sacrifice upon the cross for our sin, many turned away in unbelief.

We now know these men and women to be the majority of the nation of Israel, who seemed to truly believe in the one and only God, until of course, He came in humble human form. Spiritual blindness, coupled with the fact that they misinterpreted the scriptures, caused them to believe that He would come as an earthly king. Although nothing happens outside of God's control, this scriptural confusion played a role in the denial of Christ by the Jewish nation.

It is my opinion that history has been repeated. I am in no way suggesting that the Christian leaders of our time are duplicates of the Pharisees. I believe many are godly men who truly have good intentions, but they are well-known figures who are very rarely questioned or have their teachings disputed. Their authority is quite often strong enough to be accepted as faultless. I also believe that many prophecy teachers have made the Second Coming so complicated that it is hard to understand. Making matters worse, many of us listen to these teachers rather than search the Bible for our own answers, especially when it concerns the Second Coming. Even if we have studied His return in the Bible, we usually use one of their books to aid us.

Now, just as it was two thousand years ago, many great people are once again expecting Jesus to return in a particular way. The majority of us, as American Christians, are confident that He will come to rapture us before the persecution by the coming world leader known as the Antichrist.

In His last sermon, as recorded in Matthew, Jesus gave us the parable of the wise and foolish virgins awaiting the bridegroom. The unprepared virgins left to get more oil for their failing lamps, only to be caught off-guard and left behind, for the bridegroom returned and welcomed the virgins who were ready and waiting into the wedding banquet.

What if Christ's return doesn't happen when we think it will, or in the way we are expecting it to happen? Will we be prepared to enter the Kingdom, or will some of us have the door shut, just like the unprepared virgins? Will a portion of the Church repeat history and respond to Christ's Second Coming in the same way that the people of Israel responded to His First Coming almost two thousand years ago?

It's All About Grace

What I've learned in my prophecy studies is that the Second Coming of Jesus Christ has everything to do with grace. The moment Jesus said, "It is finished," dropped His head, and gave up His spirit, the price for every sin that every man, woman, and child has committed—or ever would commit—was paid on that terrifying, yet glorifying day.

Those who have been blessed to have God reveal this

mystery of grace to us have experienced the sanctifying work of His Spirit in our lives. The moment we raised Christ up in our hearts and said, "I am no longer the god of my life—You are," we died with Him. We became dead to sin and alive to Christ, and our walk in grace began.

Jesus, and this grace that He has freely given and lovingly lavished upon us, is our focal point. Our desires, and even our good deeds, are not to be our primary focus. Jesus Christ was crucified, arose, and supplied us with grace in abundance. This is where our eyes are to look, no matter how good or bad our lives appear to be. Once we have our hearts set in Christ's direction, then and only then can we correctly live and distribute the greatest commandment (love) by the power of God's Spirit rather than by our own efforts.

As we struggle to grasp grace, we stumble and fall, crawl and groan, always seeking to climb back to the throne of grace we had seemingly seen so clearly before. Each time we make it back to our Master's feet, we are even more thankful for what He accomplished on the cross because our understanding of our shortcomings, and His grace is broadened and clarified.

As life continues, and if it does so in accordance with His desires, our hearts become even more grateful for His sacrifice and grace as we work out our salvation with fear and trembling (Eph. 6:5).

Just as Jesus was raised on the third day, we were raised from spiritual death to spiritual life once we believed in Him. Paul tells us that because Christ was raised, we will also be physically raised before the end comes (1 Cor. 15:12–19).

The moment we are caught up in the air to be with our Lord at the Second Coming will be the first time we will fully know Jesus and His grace. Every step we have taken in this life to understand and know Him will dim in comparison to the grace we will be shown on that day. Jesus and His grace will be known more clearly than anything we have ever seen with our physical or spiritual eyes during our journey on this earth.

Imagine the moment we come face to face with Christ. I believe our lives will flash through our hearts and minds like a split-second, speed-of-light slide show. Everything we have ever done will be remembered. The evil thoughts and actions we committed against our fellow man and against God, and our infinite unworthiness, will be made known in their spiritual entirety.

As quickly as this happens, however, we will be overcome by grace. Every evil thought and deed we just viewed will be covered by the blood of the Son and fall away from us, never to be experienced again. For the first time, we will know what it means to be pure. For the first time, we will feel what it is like to be truly holy. For the first time, we will truly understand what the Father, Son, and Holy Spirit did for us on the day of the ultimate sacrifice.

We will feast with God at the great wedding banquet in celebration, for we will be Christ's bride and He our groom. From this moment on, we will live with Him, and He with us, forever. We will drink the water of life and He will wipe away every tear and take away all mourning and every ounce of pain.

We will enter the Lord's realm clothed in the righteousness of God and walk the streets of gold alongside the river of the Water of Life under God's glory, for we will no longer need a lamp or the light of the sun because He will be our light. The sting of sin that brought the curse of death will be abolished, and we will praise Him for all eternity!

Are You Ready?

Therefore, as Peter has exhorted us, let us prepare our minds for action. Let us be self-controlled, and set our hope fully on the grace to be given us when Jesus Christ is revealed (1 Peter 1:13). Study with me and see God's sovereignty and grace, and the beauty of His plan. This is much more than a look at future events. It is a journey into an area of God's heart and mind, which is fully applicable to our everyday walk with Him.

Although I don't believe the timing of the rapture to be the most important issue in Christendom, it should not be thought of as unimportant. Dive in and swim deep to discover the amazing, step-by-step guideposts God has given us. He has done this to prepare us so that we will be ready when He comes and so we will know Him better. I think you'll be surprised and eternally blessed.

By the way, I am not advocating the mid- or post-tribulation rapture theories either, for in my opinion, they also contain deficiencies. And I am certainly not a preterist who believes that Christ returned in A.D. 70. We will not give the timing of the rapture a name in this study. We will simply look at what the Bible says about this issue to show that there is no validity to a pre-tribulation rapture theory. The teaching that the Church will escape from the future suffering is man-made and purely mythical. The final generation of Christ-followers, whether it be us or others, will not avoid the persecution associated with the Antichrist.

I've written these pages with the intention of giving you a fairly in-depth Bible study. Please read along with your Bible, but if time is an issue or if you are already studying something else, feel free to just read the coming pages. I have attempted to make it an enjoyable read, even if you don't study along.

1

The Pre-Tribulation
Rapture Theory vs. The Bible

These first few pages are only here to make you think, and question the theory of the pre-tribulation rapture of the Church. I have chosen to use text from Tim LaHaye's books as examples simply because he seems to be the most famous pre-tribulation teacher at this time. Tim LaHaye the man, his integrity, and his motives will not be questioned, only his teachings and beliefs pertaining to the return of Christ. I have not addressed every scripture that I feel has been misinterpreted because I've decided not to devote the majority of my time attempting to prove men wrong but to proving the Bible right. After these few pages, the real study will begin.

Passages are from the NIV unless otherwise noted. In some sections, I have italicized portions of the scripture citations for emphasis or clarity. These italics are mine and are not in the original text.

PRE-TRIBULATION THEORY: "One of the criticisms of the pre-tribulation rapture view is that the rapture is not directly mentioned very many times in Scripture. It appears in John 14:1–3; 1 Thess. 4:13–18; 1 Cor. 15:50–56; 2 Thess. 2:1–12; and possibly Rev. 4:1–2."[3]

---

[3] *Understanding the Last Days,* Tim LaHaye, Harvest House Publishers, 1998, p. 85.

RESPONSE: The view isn't criticized because there aren't many rapture passages. The reason people like me question it is because we can't find one verse to support it. Look up the verses LaHaye just gave. Not one says we will be raptured before the Tribulation.

Here's one of the verses he just mentioned:

> Do not let your hearts be troubled. Trust in God; trust also in Me. In my Father's house are many rooms; if it were not so, I would have told you. I am going there to prepare a place for you. And if I go and prepare a place for you, I will come back and take you to be with Me that you also may be where I am. (John 14:1–3)

Does this or any other verse LaHaye mentioned say we will be raptured before the Tribulation? This is an assumption based on no biblical proof.

PRE-TRIBULATION THEORY: The Second Coming will be in two phases. First, Christ will come to rapture us in a silent, mysterious event. This could happen at any moment. The second phase of His Second Coming will be a glorious return when all will see Him.[4]

RESPONSE: In order to make their theory work, pre-trib teachers have come up with distinctions between the rapture and Christ's glorious coming, separating them by at least seven years. As we will soon see, there is no

---

[4] Paraphrased from *Are We Living in the End Times?*, Tim LaHaye and Jerry B. Jenkins, Tyndale House Publishers, Inc., 1999, pp. 98-103.

seven-year separation. In fact, this theory actually requires a Second Coming at the rapture and a Third Coming at Armageddon—although proponents of the pre-tribulation rapture call this "the two phases" of the same event.

For now, just to whet your whistle, I will give you one of the main verses used to say Christ is unseen by the world at the rapture:

> Listen, I tell you a mystery: We will not all sleep, but we will all be changed—in a flash, in the twinkling of an eye, at the last trumpet. For the trumpet will sound, the dead will be raised imperishable, and we will be changed. (1 Cor. 15:51–52)

Because this verse states that we will all be changed in a twinkling of an eye, it is taught that Christ will not be seen by the unbelieving when He returns to rapture us. This is not taking scripture at face value, even though the teachers of the pre-tribulation theory claim to be the only ones to do so. A face value interpretation tells us simply that we will all be changed "in a moment, in a twinkling of an eye." Why would Christ's return have to be invisible for that to occur? This verse states no such thing.

Look now at a verse LaHaye uses to prove the doctrine of imminence (that Christ could return at any moment and nothing must happen first):[5]

"Men of Galilee," they said, "why do you stand here looking into the sky? This same Jesus, who has been taken from you into heaven, will come back in the same way you have seen Him go into heaven." (Acts 1:11)

First of all, there is nothing here to say that we will be raptured at any moment (more on that later), and secondly, LaHaye has left out the verses before it:

After He said this, *He was taken up before their very eyes*, and a cloud hid Him from their sight. *They were looking intently up into the sky as He was going*, when suddenly two men dressed in white stood beside them. (Acts 1:9–10)

Did you notice what just happened? The very verse LaHaye used to prove that Christ could return at any moment actually proves him wrong about Christ being unseen at the rapture. Verses 9–11 say that Jesus will come back the way He left: *seen with the disciples' very eyes as He was going!* Only *after* He was seen leaving was He hidden in the clouds.

Ironically, LaHaye may have realized his error, at least on this point. In the *Tim LaHaye Prophecy Study Bible*,

---

[5] *Rapture Under Attack*, Tim LaHaye, Multnomah Publishers, Inc., 1998, p. 212.

which was published only two years after *Are We Living in the End Times?* and from which this quote was taken, LaHaye states that Acts 1:11 is *not* referring to the rapture but to "the return of Christ at the end of the seven-year Tribulation."[6]

PRE-TRIBULATION THEORY: In 2 Thess. 2:5–7, the scriptures state that there is one who holds back the man of lawlessness (the Antichrist), and this man doomed for destruction cannot be revealed until this restrainer is taken out of the way. The restrainer is the Holy Spirit. This is because the Holy Spirit will be taken out of the way when the Church is raptured because He is in the Church and He will go with them. Then the seven-year Tribulation can begin.

RESPONSE: Almost all pre-trib teachers say this. LaHaye states, "When the church is raptured at the beginning of the Tribulation, the Holy Spirit, Who dwells in the church, will be gone."[7] It is interesting to note that in 1975, he was just as dogmatic when he wrote, "The restrainer in this passage is not the Holy Spirit; the reference is to three of the kings of the revived

---

[6] *Tim LaHaye Prophecy Study Bible*, Tim LaHaye, AMG Publishers, 2000, p. 1164.

[7] *Rapture Under Attack*, p. 113.

Roman Empire...."[8] He doesn't give a single verse to back up either claim.

So, is the restrainer the Holy Spirit? Is the Holy Spirit removed before the Tribulation? Mark 13:9–11 states that we will be brought before the governors, councils, and kings to be put on trial and beaten in the times of persecution by the Antichrist. However, we are told not to worry because at that time, the Holy Spirit will give us the words to say. Matthew 24:22, 31 also makes it clear that the elect of God will be persecuted by the Antichrist during the Tribulation. If the elect have the Holy Spirit in them, which we all do, how could the Spirit be gone if we are still on earth?

Also, nowhere in the Bible does it say the Holy Spirit's job is to restrain wickedness. His job is to convict the world of sin (John 16:8). He also regenerates (John 3:5), guides (John 16:13), counsels (John 14:26), intercedes (Romans 8:26), sanctifies (Romans 15:16), and much more, but the Bible says nothing about restraining wickedness. And, if the Holy Spirit's job is to convict the world of sin, how can people come to Christ during the 70th Week of Daniel if the Holy Spirit is not there to make them *aware* of their sin? After all, LaHaye and most pre-trib advocates teach that there will be a great revival after the rapture.

These points have been made known to pre-trib

---

[8] *Revelation Illustrated And Made Plain*, Tim LaHaye, Lamplighter Books, Revised Edition 1975, p. 112.

teachers in recent years. Because of this, they now say that *most* of the Holy Spirit is removed. I would add that, even if, by a one-in-a-thousand chance, the Holy Spirit *is* the restrainer, why would the Church have to be raptured in order for Him to remove His restraining power? To believe this would be a huge assumption.

PRE-TRIBULATION THEORY: The Church is the restrainer of 2 Thessalonians, and once we are taken out of the way in the rapture, the Antichrist can be revealed to begin the Tribulation.

RESPONSE: Some (excluding LaHaye) also say this, but in the Bible, the Church is the Bride of Christ and always female in gender (Eph. 5:25, Rev. 19:7, 21:9). The restrainer of 2 Thessalonians is referred to as "he."

PRE-TRIBULATION THEORY: The Church is not mentioned even *once* in Revelation chapters 4–18 because we are raptured before the Tribulation.[9]

RESPONSE: In many of his books, LaHaye informs us that the word "saints" rather than "church" is used to speak of the Christ-followers in Revelation 4–18 because the Church is not on earth at this time. The reason, he says, is that we are raptured beforehand. He jumps to

---

[9] *Understanding the Last Days*, p. 94.

conclusions by boldly stating, "The church is not mentioned even *once*." This is a very short-sighted view
because the truth of the matter is that only the *word*
"church" is not mentioned. This is a far cry from the
actual Church itself not being mentioned.

Okay, so the word "church" isn't used in these chapters. The word "saints" is used instead. Is this because the
Church isn't there due to a pre-trib rapture? The word
"saints" is found in the NIV New Testament 33 times
before the book of Revelation. *Every single time*, it refers
to those who are of the Church, as in 2 Cor. 1:1: "To the
church of God in Corinth, together with all the saints
throughout Achaia...." If "saints" refers to the Church in
every instance *before* Revelation, there is no reason it is
not speaking of the Church *in* Revelation.

It is also important to keep in mind that the word
"church" is not mentioned in the end of Revelation during the thousand-year reign of Christ or the times of the
New Jerusalem either. Does the absence of this word
mean we are not there? Of course not. Furthermore,
John, the recorder of Revelation, never used the word
"church" in the books of John or 1 John, which he also
wrote. The argument from silence concerning the word
"church" is beyond unconvincing.

PRE-TRIBULATION THEORY: "After John is called
up into heaven and the world goes through the
Tribulation period, the Church is not mentioned even

once until [Revelation] chapter 19, when she is seen coming with Christ to rule and reign with Him."[10]

RESPONSE: This is a great example of how the pre-tribulation rapture theory is filled with all sorts of assumptions. It is taught that we will return with Christ in Rev. 19:14 to fight with Him at the battle of Armageddon, but Rev. 19:14 doesn't say this. It says that *armies* (not the Church), wearing linen that is *white and clean* (NAS), are seen coming with Christ to this battle (Rev. 19:19).

The assumption is made that these armies are the Church because Rev. 19:8 says that the saints are given linen that is "bright and clean" (NAS). It overlooks the fact that Rev. 15:6 states that angels wear linen that is "clean and bright" (NAS).[11] Furthermore, 2 Thess. 1:7–8 tells us that angels return with Christ to deal out retribution. The armies seen in Rev. 19:14 appear to be angels, not the Church. Not one verse says that the Church will return with Christ as the pre-trib doctrine claims as fact.

(Notice the irony here? LaHaye criticizes other rapture views for seeing the Church in Revelation 5–18 even though the word "church" is not used, but he is doing the exact same thing in this argument!)

This is also one of the many assumptions made that ends up manipulating scripture to make it appear that we will avoid persecution. According to this argument,

---

[10] *Understanding the Last Days*, p. 94.

[11] *The Sign*, Robert Van Kampen, Crossway Books, Third Revised Edition, 2000, pp. 415-416.

because we are seen returning with Christ to battle at Armageddon in Rev. 19:14 (which no passage supports), we *must* be raptured pre-tribulationally and then wait in heaven for seven years for the battle.[12] This is not true.

And even if the Church is the army of Rev. 19:14, there is no need for the rapture to take place seven years beforehand. A rapture shortly before the battle would work just as well.

PRE-TRIBULATION THEORY: Matthew 24 is not applicable to the rapture of the saints. In fact, it is not applicable to the Church in general because it was written for Israel, not the Church. (Some pre-tribulation scholars will even argue that *all* of Matthew was written only for Israel because it was written for the Jews to answer their questions about the Messiah.)

RESPONSE: The Bible says this? No, the pre-tribulation teachers have said this to keep Matthew 24 out of their debate. If Matthew 24 is included in their teachings, their doctrines will crumble.

If what they say is true, who gets to make up the rules for deciding which teachings are for the Church and which are exclusively for Israel? Sure, there are cases in which certain passages refer specifically to Israel rather than to the Church and vice versa, but when studied closely within the context, it is apparent which are

---

12 *Rapture Under Attack*, p. 212.

which. It is only when *all* scriptures pertaining to a certain subject are compared, without throwing any verses away, that a correct conclusion can be made.

Furthermore, if Matthew 24 is only for Israel, and *no* distinctions are made to tell us that this chapter is different from the rest of the book, then *all* of Matthew must be for Israel. Here is where the problem begins. If all of Matthew is for Israel only, then all of Mark and Luke are only for Israel too, because the Olivet Discourse in Matthew 24 is found in Mark and Luke as well.

Also, Matt. 28:19–20 is the Great Commission. Robert Van Kampen has argued that Jesus tells His disciples to go to all nations and teach them to observe *all* He had commanded them. Teach them everything. Not, "All except for what I told you concerning the end—teach that only to Israel."[13] Why then, when Jesus is speaking to the disciples in Matthew 1–23 and 25–28, do we apply it to us, but in Chapter 24, we accept it when the teachers tell us that it doesn't? This defies basic logic.

Not only this, but Jesus is talking to His disciples who were—or at least were soon to become—the Church, depending upon how one views it. Either way, the disciples were Christ-followers who had everything to do with the Church. In fact, Peter, James, and John would be called "pillars" of the Church in the not-too-distant future (Gal. 2:9). I tend to think that *who* Jesus is talking to would carry more weight than *to whom* the book

---

[13] *The Rapture Question Answered: Plain & Simple*, Robert Van Kampen, Fleming H. Revell, 1997, pp. 102-105.

was written. In this instance, I would say that He is speaking to both the Church and the Jewish nation, Israel. Whoever has an ear, let him hear.

Last, and certainly not least, did you know that Matthew is the only gospel that refers to the Church using the actual word "church" (Matt. 16:18; 18:17)? Why would that be if the book were only written for Israel?

PRE-TRIBULATION THEORY: Matthew 24:36 "Warn[s] against attempts to set an exact date for the rapture."[14]

> No one knows about that day or hour, not even the angels in heaven, nor the Son, but only the Father. (Matt. 24:36)

RESPONSE: Finally we agree on something! No one knows the day or the hour. But wait! This verse is found in Matthew 24, and LaHaye (like most pre-trib teachers) says Matthew 24 is not applicable in a rapture conversation because this chapter is only concerning the time *after* we are raptured. This is a contradiction.

PRE-TRIBULATION THEORY: According to LaHaye's Web site, the purpose of the rapture is clear within pre-tribulationism. He states, "It is a needed event to remove the Church so that God can complete His

---

[14] *Tim LaHaye Prophecy Study Bible*, p. 1040.

unfinished program for Israel that will result in her conversion and eventual Millennial blessings."[15]

RESPONSE: God *needs* this event to happen so He *can* work in Israel? God isn't big enough to work in the Church and Israel at the same time?

PRE-TRIBULATION THEORY: "Concerning the rapture of the Church...It may occur at any moment. There is no prophesied event that must take place before the Lord Jesus returns for all believers."[16]

RESPONSE: Here are some of the many verses taught within the pre-tribulation camp to show that Christ could come at any moment and that nothing has to happen first: Titus 2:13, 1 John 3:2–3, John 14:1–3, Acts 1:11, 1 Cor.1:7, 1 Cor. 15:51–52, Phil. 3:20, Col. 3:4, and 1 Thess. 5:6. Look up the verses and discover just a small piece of how pre-tribulation teachers come up with their doctrines. They assume much.

Where in these verses does it say Christ will return at any moment and that nothing has to happen first? Nowhere. In fact, Acts 1:11, one of the verses LaHaye and countless other teachers use to try to prove their imminence doctrine,[17] says quite the opposite:

"Men of Galilee," they said, "why do you stand

---

[15] www.timlahaye.com/about_ministry/index.php3?p=faq&section=FAQs

[16] *Tim LaHaye Prophecy Study Bible*, p. 1166.

[17] *Rapture Under Attack*, p. 212.

here looking into the sky? This same Jesus, who
has been taken from you into heaven, will come
back in the same way you have seen him go into
heaven." (Acts1:11)

Does this teach imminence? Hardly. It simply says that
Jesus will come back in the same way He was taken up
into heaven. So, to prove that the rapture will take place
at any moment, these teachers must also take the position that the ascension could have happened at any
moment and that the rapture at His Second Coming will
be the same.

Now we see how illogical this argument really is.
Nothing had to happen before the ascension? He didn't
have to die and be raised from the dead before He could
ascend? No, this passage simply says that Jesus will be
seen in glory at the Second Coming.

Soon, we will see for ourselves as we examine the
Bible that the doctrine of imminence is not found and
that we who truly want to know the truth have been
misled. The pre-trib teachers simply refuse to accept
that the Church's persecution by the Antichrist is the
prophesied event that must take place before the rapture
at Christ's return.

PRE-TRIBULATION THEORY: We are supposed to
want Christ to return. To say we won't be raptured before
the Tribulation and will have to face persecution before
He returns makes no sense. If we have to be persecuted

first, why would we want Him to come back?

RESPONSE: If the pre-tribulation argument holds water, then we must ask this question: Why did Jesus want to come to this God-forsaken planet if He knew He would have to be mocked, whipped, beaten beyond recognition, and nailed to a cross for half a day? Because it was His Father's will.

> My Father, if it is possible, may this cup be taken from Me. Yet not as I will, but as You will. (Matt. 26:39)

No, access to glory by the way of persecution doesn't make sense if we use the human thought process. If we use this frame of mind, we miss the fact that God, not our circumstances, is our comfort and security. The world does not revolve around us. The most important thing is not that He is here for us. It is that we are here for Him. We were put here to worship the Almighty Creator in the way that He desires: whole-heartedly to glorify Him. The mature follower of Christ finds peace and joy in the midst of suffering (Acts 5:41, Romans 5:3, 1 Peter 4:12–19). If we use the mind of Christ, which He has given to all who believe (1 Cor. 2:6–16), we will want His will to be accomplished, no matter the cost.

PRE-TRIBULATION THEORY: "Pre-tribulation Christians are looking for the coming of the Lord. Other views have them awaiting Tribulation, the Antichrist, and suffering."[18]

RESPONSE: Once again, if we use human reasoning, this is what we will conclude. Acts 5:40–42 tells us that the apostles were flogged 39 times and told not to speak in Jesus' name. What did they do? Did they walk through life focusing on the potential beatings and keep their mouths shut? Of course not. They rejoiced because they were worthy to suffer for Jesus and then continued teaching and proclaiming the good news because they understood how to use the spiritual eyes God gave them rather than their physical eyes.

Yes, we should know of the coming persecution so that we will be prepared, but we are told to think about whatever is true, noble, right, pure, lovely, admirable, excellent, and praiseworthy (Phil. 4:8). We are to focus on good and God, not evil and Satan.

PRE-TRIBULATION THEORY: "It [the pre-tribulation rapture theory] is the only view that makes 'the blessed hope' truly a blessed hope. Remember: Rapture teaching was given to comfort those who mourn! The threat of going through the Tribulation is hardly a doctrine of comfort to the saints."[19] And, "If Christ does not rapture His church before the Tribulation begins, much of the hope is

---

[18] *Rapture Under Attack*, p. 212.

[19] *Rapture Under Attack*, p. 211.

destroyed, and thus it becomes a blasted hope."[20]

RESPONSE: Blasted hope? This statement makes my neck hair stand on end! If Tim LaHaye is wrong in his theology, he has just called Christ's return a blasted hope! Remember, LaHaye and his fellow teachers tell us that Jesus will be unseen by the world at the rapture and then seen only later at His glorious appearance.

This "blessed hope" LaHaye refers to throughout *Rapture Under Attack* is found in Titus 2:13:

> ...looking for the blessed hope and the appearing of the glory of our great God and Savior, Jesus Christ. (NASB)

According to the pre-tribulation teaching, the "blessed hope" mentioned in this verse is referring to the rapture at Christ's invisible return, and the "appearing of the glory of our great God and Savior, Jesus Christ" is referring to the visible appearance of Christ approximately seven years later at the end of the Tribulation. This is used as proof of the difference between the rapture at the invisible coming and His glorious return.

Titus 2:10–13 instructs us to live godly lives and to look for "the blessed hope" *and* "the appearing of the glory." If the rapture is the blessed hope and is approxi-

---

[20] *Rapture Under Attack*, p. 69.

31

mately seven years before the "appearing of the glory," how can we look for the appearing if we are raptured more than seven years earlier? When this verse is interpreted literally, it is not possible to suggest that Titus 2:13 shows both the rapture and the glorious appearing as two separate events as pre-tribulation teachers suggest.

Also, LaHaye sure makes it sound as if he has put an awful lot of hope into being raptured and saved from suffering under the hand of the Antichrist. I sincerely hope that none of us has more faith in our circumstances than hope in Christ. I thought we were supposed to place our hope in Jesus and the grace God has freely given and lavished upon us, and on the fact that this grace will be made evident when we meet the Lord to be with Him forever.

> Let us fix our eyes on Jesus…. (Heb. 12:2)

> Therefore, prepare your minds for action; be self-controlled; set your hope fully on the grace to be given you when Jesus Christ is revealed. (1 Peter 1:13)

I believe that the glorious appearing is the blessed hope because we will see our Savior face to face and because of the grace to be given us at that time. This is enough to keep me satisfied and more than enough in which to place my hope.

2

The Second Coming of Christ and the Day of the Lord

Now, let's take a closer look at the Second Coming of Christ and the Day of the Lord. In order to do this, we need to define several terms. First, we will start with the term "coming."

<u>COMING</u> = _Parousia_ (Greek): noun; present, presence, being present.

The term "coming," as used concerning Christ's Second Coming, is always _parousia_ (Strong's 3952), a noun. If it were a verb, "coming" would be the simple activity of Jesus coming from there to here. "Coming" being a noun makes it a person, place, or thing. It is obviously not a person or place, so it must be a thing.

It is a thing—an event—like Jesus' First Coming. He didn't simply come from heaven to earth and that was it. He came as an infant, grew up, taught, loved, died, rose, and ascended. All aspects of His 33-year life were part of the First Coming. As we will see during the study, the Second Coming is likewise. It spans an unknown time period containing many occurrences. _Parousia_ means to come and stay, a continuing presence.

"Coming," when speaking of the Second Coming, can

refer to Christ's coming to deliver us at the rapture, as in 1 Thess 4:15–17; or it can refer to His coming to deliver wrath upon the world as in 2 Peter 3:4–7. And, as we will soon find after studying together, "coming" can speak of deliverance of the saints and the pouring out of God's wrath upon the ungodly at the same time.

The next term is "the Day of the Lord."

<u>DAY OF THE LORD</u> = the wrath of God poured out in the end time on those who refuse to repent.

The Day of the Lord is a day of judgment (Isa. 2:13–17), justice (Obadiah 15), destruction (Joel 1:15), vengeance (Jer. 46:10), punishment (Zeph. 1:8), battle (Eze. 13:5, Zech. 14:3), and panic (Isa. 22:5).

> But that day belongs to the Lord, the LORD Almighty— a day of vengeance, for vengeance on his foes. The sword will devour till it is satisfied, till it has quenched its thirst with blood. For the Lord, the LORD Almighty, will offer sacrifice in the land of the north by the River Euphrates. (Jer. 46:10)

> Alas for that day! For the day of the LORD is near; it will come like destruction from the Almighty. (Joel 1:15)

While most references to the "Day" in Isaiah, Jeremiah, Amos, and Zephaniah are to wrath and judgment, Joel speaks much concerning the deliverance of faithful and repentant Israel (who remains after the Church is "caught up"/raptured because of her unbelief prior to this event). For the purposes of studying the rapture, however, wrath is how we should view the Day of the Lord.

The word "day" in the Bible can mean a literal day, as in Psalms 84:10: "Better is one day in your courts than a thousand elsewhere; I would rather be a doorkeeper in the house of my God than dwell in the tents of the wicked." Or, it can refer to an unknown, longer period of time, as in Isa. 4:2: "In that day the Branch of the Lord will be beautiful and glorious, and the fruit of the land will be the pride and glory of the survivors in Israel."

The "day" in the Day of the Lord is the latter. We do not know exactly when it will start or how long it will last. What we do know is this: It begins at the *parousia* of the Lord (and consequently, the rapture), and there will be a sign given in the sky before it begins.

> The sun will be turned to darkness and the moon to blood *before* the coming of the great and dreadful day of the LORD. (Joel 2:31)

And, in Isaiah, we are told that the Lord will be the only one exalted during this Day:

> The eyes of the arrogant man will be humbled and the pride of men brought low; the Lord alone will be exalted in that day. (Isaiah 2:11)

3

Matthew 24: The Foundation

Let me begin by saying that I confidently believe that *anyone* can read and understand the Bible if they dig in and study. One should not *need* to study Greek to understand the Bible, but because of the disagreements I have with the pre-trib doctrine, some Greek words will be evaluated in order to show some interesting points. If you have questions about these words, I encourage you to get a *Strong's Concordance* and a Bible with a Greek parallel and lexicon. I believe you'll be surprised by just how much you can understand and learn. I know you'll find it very gratifying. Now let's begin walking through this very important chapter.

In this chapter, Jesus has just left the temple and is walking away when His disciples come up to Him to call His attention to its buildings. But instead of joining the discussion of the buildings' majesty, Jesus says, "Do you see all these things? I tell you the truth, not one stone here will be left on another; every one will be thrown down" (Matthew 24:2).

The disciples were shocked. Later, as Jesus was sitting on the Mount of Olives, the disciples came to Him privately and said, "Tell us, when will this happen, and what will be the sign of Your coming and of the end of the age?"

As you read Christ's response, make sure you take notice of the fact that there is no rapture of any kind mentioned before the troubled times associated with the Antichrist.

Jesus replied:

> Watch out that no one deceives you. For many will come in my name, claiming, "I am the Christ," and will deceive many. You will hear of wars and rumors of wars, but see to it that you are not alarmed. Such things must happen, but the end is still to come. Nation will rise against nation, and kingdom against kingdom. There will be famines and earthquakes in various places. All these are the beginning of birth pains.

> Then you will be handed over to be persecuted and put to death, and you will be hated by all nations because of Me. At that time many will turn away from the faith and will betray and hate each other, and many false prophets will appear and deceive many people. Because of the increase of wickedness, the love of most will grow cold, but he who stands firm to the end will be saved. And this gospel of the kingdom will be preached in the whole world as a testimony to all nations, and then the end will come.

> So when you see standing in the holy place "the abomination that causes desolation," spoken of through the prophet Daniel—let the reader understand—then let those who are in Judea flee to the mountains. Let no one on the roof of his

house go down to take anything out of the house. Let no one in the field go back to get his cloak. How dreadful it will be in those days for pregnant women and nursing mothers! Pray that your flight will not take place in winter or on the Sabbath. For then there will be great distress, unequaled from the beginning of the world until now, and never to be equaled again. If those days had not been cut short, no one would survive, but for the sake of the elect those days will be shortened.

At that time if anyone says to you, "Look, here is the Christ!" or, "There He is!" do not believe it. For false Christs and false prophets will appear and perform great signs and miracles to deceive even the elect—if that were possible. See, I have told you ahead of time. So if anyone tells you, "There He is, out in the desert," do not go out; or, "Here He is, in the inner rooms," do not believe it. For as lightning that comes from the east is visible even in the west, so will be the coming of the Son of Man. Wherever there is a carcass, there the vultures will gather.

Immediately after the distress of those days, the sun will be darkened, and the moon will not give its light; the stars will fall from the sky, and the heavenly bodies will be shaken.

At that time the sign of the Son of Man will appear in the sky, and all the nations of the earth will mourn. They will see the Son of Man coming

on the clouds of the sky, with power and great
glory. And He will send His angels with a loud
trumpet call, and they will gather His elect from
the four winds, from one end of the heavens to
the other. (Matt. 24:1–31)

Remember, the pre-trib teachers would have us
believe that the coming of Christ described in this passage is His coming at Armageddon, not at the rapture. If
this is the case, then the rapture must have occurred
sometime during this discussion. This leads us to an
interesting question. Of all the signs Jesus gave His disciples so that believers would know when the end was
near, why didn't He tell them that a bunch of people
would suddenly disappear? The pre-trib theory teaches
that the increase of earthquakes, famines, and wars are
signs that take place before the rapture. Those would be
pretty hard to judge if they were spread out over a large
period of time like the pre-trib theory claims. Wouldn't
Christ have told the Jewish nation to look for an obvious
sign like the rapture before the persecution if Matthew
was only written for Israel?

Let's Compare

Now let's read about the battle of Armageddon in Rev.
19:11–21 and compare it with the description in
Matthew 24:

I saw heaven standing open and there before me was a white horse, whose rider is called Faithful and True. With justice He judges and makes war. His eyes are like blazing fire, and on His head are many crowns. He has a name written on Him that no one knows but He Himself. He is dressed in a robe dipped in blood, and His name is the Word of God. The armies of heaven were following Him, riding on white horses and dressed in fine linen, white and clean. Out of His mouth comes a sharp sword with which to strike down the nations. He will rule them with an iron scepter. He treads the winepress of the fury of the wrath of God Almighty. On His robe and on His thigh He has this name written:

KING OF KINGS AND LORD OF LORDS.

And I saw an angel standing in the sun, who cried in a loud voice to all the birds flying in midair, "Come, gather together for the great supper of God, so that you may eat the flesh of kings, generals, and mighty men, of horses and their riders, and the flesh of all people, free and slave, small and great."

Then I saw the beast and the kings of the earth and their armies gathered together to make war against the rider on the horse and His army. But the beast was captured, and with him the false prophet who had performed the miraculous signs on his behalf. With these signs he had deluded those who had received the mark of the

> beast and worshiped his image. The two of them
> were thrown alive into the fiery lake of burning
> sulfur. The rest of them were killed with the
> sword that came out of the mouth of the rider on
> the horse, and all the birds gorged themselves on
> their flesh. (Rev. 19:11–21)

Do you see a comparison between Matt. 24:29–31 and Rev. 19:11–21? Probably not, but the coming in Matthew 24 is what the pre-tribulation teachers say is Armageddon, which we just read, in order to avoid the conclusion that the rapture occurs at Christ's coming *after* the persecution.

Now that you see the difference between the coming of Christ described in Matthew 24 and His descent from heaven at Armageddon, and recall the earlier debate about Matthew 24 as being for the Church as well as for Israel, let's proceed to see if what I have been saying is true. I will do my best to take everything one step at a time, but please use your Bible along with what I have prepared for you. This is meant to be a Bible study.

The Layout

Matthew 24:2 begins by Jesus telling His disciples,

> ...not one stone here will be left on another, every
> one will be thrown down.

41

Jesus said this in reference to the temple they were all gazing upon in verse one. This temple Jesus was talking about, and foreseeing being torn down, was demolished soon after. In A.D. 70, His prediction came true.

Notice that Matthew only records Christ's answer to the disciples about the sign of His coming and the end times, not their question about the demolition of the temple. If you're curious about what Jesus says about the destruction of the temple, see Luke 21:5–36.[21]

After asking about the temple, the disciples asked Jesus this question:

> "Tell us," they said, "*when will this happen*, and *what will be the sign of your coming and of the end of the age?*" (Matt. 24:3)

Jesus then begins telling them what they want to know. Notice my italics in the verse above and see as we continue that Jesus is speaking about *when* the destruction in the end times will happen and *what the sign of His coming and of the end of the age* will be, not addressing the end of the temple and Jerusalem.

---

[21] For a very brief explanation concerning the destruction of the temple, open your Bible to Luke 21:8, where Jesus begins speaking about the end times. In verse 12, notice that He says, "Before all this [in other words, before the end-times events He was just talking about]." He then tells of Jerusalem's destruction in verses 12–24 and resumes speaking of His coming and the end in 25–36.

In verses 4–8, we read about the birth pains that must take place before the end. Jesus said,

> Watch out that no one deceives you. For many will come in my name, claiming, 'I am the Christ,' and will deceive many. You will hear of wars and rumors of wars, but see to it that you are not alarmed. Such things must happen, but the end is still to come. Nation will rise against nation, and kingdom against kingdom. There will be famines and earthquakes in various places. All these are the beginning of birth pains. (Matt. 24:4–8)

Verses 9–10 begin to reveal the persecution and death of Christ's followers that will take place, along with the turning away from the faith that is the apostasy (we will look into the apostasy later):

> Then you will be handed over to be persecuted and put to death, and you will be hated by all nations because of Me. At that time many will turn away from the faith and will betray and hate each other. (Matt. 24:9–10)

Verse 15 tells us what causes the persecution, death, and apostasy: the abomination that causes desolation.

> So when you see standing in the holy place "the abomination that causes desolation," spoken of through the prophet Daniel,...(Matt. 24:15)

This refers to the man of lawlessness, or the Antichrist, and his detestable action of setting himself up in the temple of God, claiming to be God at the midpoint of the 70th Week. More about this later, too.

Then, we read:

> For then [when the abomination stands in the holy place—v. 15] there will be great distress unequaled from the beginning of the world until now—and never to be equaled again. If those days had not been cut short, no one would survive, but for the sake of the elect, those days will be shortened. (Matt. 24:21–22)

Those days will be shortened? What does that mean? The days of distress, or tribulation, caused by the Antichrist will be shortened for the elect because of the rapture! We will soon see if this is correct.

Let's Begin

Now is when our study truly begins. Dig deep and keep an open mind, but don't take *my* word for it. Throw away any preconceptions you may have and search the scriptures with all your heart. If you make it to the end, you will be one of the very few who uncover one of the most amazing prophecies ever given.

Now, for a moment, look at the two classic rapture passages everyone agrees on. My italics show the phrases referring to the rapture.

According to the Lord's own word, we tell you that we who are still alive, who are left until the *coming* [*parousia*] of the Lord, will certainly not precede those who have fallen asleep. For the Lord Himself will come down from heaven, with a loud command, with the voice of the archangel and with the trumpet call of God, and the dead in Christ will rise first. After that, *we who are still alive and are left will be caught up together with them in the clouds to meet the Lord in the air.* And so we will be with the Lord forever. (1 Thess. 4:15–17)

Concerning the coming [*parousia*] of our Lord Jesus Christ and *our being gathered to Him*....(2 Thess 2:1)

These two passages just referred to Christ's coming using the noun *parousia*, which we spoke of earlier. They also make it clear that His coming/*parousia* is related to the rapture, or our "being gathered" (or being "caught up") to Him.

Now, let's compare scripture with scripture and see where "coming/*parousia*" is located in Matthew 24:

For as lightning that comes from the east is visible even in the west, so will be the coming [*parousia*] of the Son of Man. Wherever there is a carcass, there the vultures will gather.

Immediately after the distress [caused by the abomination; vv. 15, 21] of those days the sun will be darkened, and the moon will not give its light; the stars will fall from the sky, and the heavenly bodies will be shaken.

At that time the sign of the Son of Man will appear in the sky, and all the nations of the earth will mourn. They will see the Son of Man coming on the clouds of the sky, with power and great glory. And He will send His angels with a loud trumpet call, and they will gather His elect from the four winds, from one end of the heavens to the other. (Matt. 24:27–31)

The "coming/*parousia*" found in 1 and 2 Thessalonians concerning the rapture (being caught up, gathering) is found *after* the sign of the sun, moon, and stars in Matt. 24:30, which is also *after* the abomination that causes desolation (v. 15) and the persecution.

Notice the loud trumpet call in Matt. 24:31. Now notice the trumpet call of God in the rapture passage in 1 Thessalonians we just read. Also notice the *gathering* of His elect in Matt. 24:31, as in the *gathering* in the rapture passage in 2 Thess. 2:1. The rapture is a part of the coming/*parousia* of Christ, which takes place after the sign in the sun, moon, and stars. The rapture is not seven years before the coming as we have been taught by the pre-tribulation doctrine.

Now let's look in Luke for added information and verification concerning the coming found in the Olivet Discourse in Matthew 24:

There will be signs in the sun, moon and stars.…
At that time they will see the Son of Man coming
in a cloud with power and great glory. When
these things begin to take place, stand up and lift
up your heads, because your redemption is
drawing near. (Luke 21:25–28)

When we see the sign in the sun, moon, and stars, we
are told to lift up our heads. Why? Because our redemption is drawing near! Look up! Christ is coming and we
will be gathered to Him forever!

"But wait!" you have probably already said to yourself.
"Are you trying to tell me things must happen first, and
that there will be signs? The Bible says the rapture will
come like a thief in the night. All the movies say it, and
most of the songs say it."

Yes, all the movies and songs say it, and the pre-tribulation doctrine screams that Christ could return at any
moment, but the Bible does not say it. I know it is hard
to believe. At one time, I thought it was heresy when I
heard people say this, but please, continue to study with
me and the proof will be revealed time and time again.

The Boat With Meaning

I have a question for you. To whom will Christ's coming
be like a thief? To us? Will something be taken from us?
No, we will be taken from them! Let's read on in
Matthew 24 and see what Jesus really says about this

47

matter. He correlates the deliverance of Noah by God in the ark with the deliverance of the elect in the rapture at His coming. Also correlated is the wrath of God at the flood and the wrath at His Second Coming.

> No one knows about that day or hour, not even the angels in heaven, nor the Son, but only the Father. As it was in the days of Noah, so it will be at the coming of the Son of Man. For in the days before the flood, people were eating and drinking, marrying and giving in marriage, up to the day Noah entered the ark, and they knew nothing about what would happen until the flood came and took them all away. That is how it will be at the coming of the Son of Man. (Matt. 24:36–39)

Do you see the parallel? The coming of the Son of Man will be like the days of Noah. Noah was delivered by the ark being swept away, then God's wrath came. The elect will be delivered by the rapture sweeping us away, then God's wrath will come. They (wrath recipients at the flood) knew nothing about what would happen until it did. They (wrath recipients at the coming/ *parousia*) won't know either.

God's judgment comes as a thief to unbelievers, not to believers. Noah certainly knew what would soon happen. God told him! And He's telling us, too! If Jesus wasn't telling us what will happen before He comes, why in the world would He say that He's told us everything in advance, and that we should therefore be on guard?

> So be on your guard; I have told you everything
> ahead of time. (Mark 13:23)

This Noah correlation again verifies that the rapture is a part of the coming. Furthermore, the Noah parallel tells us that the wrath of God is also connected to His coming and will take place at the rapture. Remember, the wrath at the flood came as Noah was being delivered.

We already saw in Matt. 24:29–31 that after the distress (caused by the abomination), the sun will darken, the moon will turn to blood, and the stars will fall. The Son of Man will be seen coming, the trumpet will be blown, and the gathering of the elect will occur. This coming/*parousia* in Matt. 24:29–31 is the same coming that Jesus said would be like the days of Noah. The Noah parallel doubly confirms that Jesus is talking about the rapture, then wrath, at the coming/*parousia*.

Once again, Luke adds information:

> Just as it was in the days of Noah, so also will it
> be in the days of the Son of Man. People were
> eating, drinking, marrying and being given in
> marriage up to the day Noah entered the ark.
> Then the flood came and destroyed them all.
> (Luke 17:26–27)

> It was the same in the days of Lot. People were
> eating and drinking, buying and selling, planting
> and building. But the day Lot left Sodom, fire and
> sulfur rained down from heaven and destroyed
> them all. (Luke 17:28–29)

49

The day of Lot and the days of the Son of Man are likened to one another. Lot left Sodom (we will leave the earth), and then the wrath came (the Day of the Lord will come). Remember, this coming that Jesus is relating to the day of Lot is after the persecution and after the sign of the sun, moon, and stars.

Verses 39–41 of Matthew 24 confirm for a third time that Jesus is talking about the rapture at His coming:

> That is how it will be at the coming of the Son of Man. Two men will be in the field, one will be taken and the other left. Two women will be grinding with a hand mill, one will be taken and the other left. (Matt. 24:39–41)

Remember, the coming Jesus describes in verses 39–41 is the same coming that He describes only a few verses earlier, in verses 27–31, which is after the sign of the sun, moon, and stars. This confirms it for a third time. The Noah parallel is not only talking about the surprise of the godless, but the rapture and wrath, too.

Most Christians who believe in the pre-trib theory also use verses 39–41 as a rapture passage, but they are unaware that, in the pre-trib view, this is a contradiction. If the gathering of the elect at Christ's coming is not the rapture in verses 29–31 (as pre-trib teaches), how can it be the rapture only a few verses later, in verses 39–41? One can't be Armageddon and the other the rapture. They are both talking about the same event.

Some teachers of the pre-tribulation doctrine get

around this problem by saying that those taken in verses 39–41 are not the raptured elect. Rather, they are the godless taken away to destruction at the battle of Armageddon because in the preceding verse, the objects of God's wrath were taken away in the flood. They teach that the ones left are those who came to Christ during the 70th Week of Daniel (after the pre-trib rapture) and are alive to remain for the thousand-year reign of Christ on earth. This does not add up.

If those "taken" in Matt. 24:39–41 are taken to judgment because those at the time of Noah were taken away to judgment, who do we have left? Those who are left behind. Was Noah left behind? This teaching is supposed to line up with the times of Noah because, as Jesus said, "Just as it was in the days of Noah, so also will it be in the days of the Son of Man."

For the times of Noah to truly parallel the times of Christ's return, those "taken" in Matt. 24: 40-41 must be the raptured elect and those "left" must be those left behind for God's judgment. After all, this is the way it happened so many years ago. Noah was rescued and the enemies of God were left behind.

Also, the Greek word used to tell of the godless being taken away in wrath at the flood in verse 39 is *airo* (Strong's 142), which simply means "taken away" or "carried away." The original Greek word "taken," seen in verse 40, is *paralambano* (Strong's 3880), which means: "to take," or "receive near." It doesn't make sense to say that the objects of His wrath are received near, because they are not. We are.

In fact, this word, *paralambano*, is also found in John:

> And if I go and prepare a place for you, I will
> come again, and *receive* you to Myself; that where
> I am, there you may be also. (John 14:3—NAS)

The word *paralambano* is an intimate word used by
Jesus to tell us that He will take us near to Him at His
coming. This statement in John 14:3 was made one day
after the Olivet Discourse in Matthew 24.

While many people point out that *paralambano* may
be used to describe one being received near for something other than intimacy, as Jesus was received for
mockery and abuse in Matt. 27:27, it doesn't fit in this
context. As we read above, if those "taken" (*paralambano*) in verses 39–41 are those taken to wrath, as pre-
trib teachers would have us believe, the passage and the
Lord's return no longer parallel the days of Noah.

Matthew 24:40–41 is clearly speaking of the saints
being taken to Him in the rapture, not the godless being
taken away to destruction:

> Therefore keep watch, because you do not know
> on what day your Lord will come. But under-
> stand this: If the owner of the house had known
> at what time of night the thief was coming, he
> would have kept watch and would not have let
> his house be broken into. So you also must be
> ready, because the Son of Man will come at an
> hour when you do not expect Him. (Matt.
> 24:42–45)

As we just saw in verses 42–45, we don't know the day or the hour He will come, but that does not require that Christ could return at any moment. It doesn't say we won't know the decade He will come. It does not state that there are no prophesied events that must happen first. Even Jesus didn't know the day or the hour (v. 36), but He obviously knew the signs that would precede His coming. He just told us in verses 4–29!

Further confirmation, showing us the "day and hour" statement made by Jesus is a general reference and does not speak of an "any moment" return, is found in the following passage:

> Even so, when you see all these things, you know that it is near, right at the door. I tell you the truth, this generation will certainly not pass away until all these things have happened. (Matt. 24:33–34)

"This generation," of course, is not speaking of the generation Jesus is talking to at the time, for if it were, Jesus would be wrong because that generation didn't see "all these things." "This generation" refers to the generation that sees all the things happening that Jesus is talking about (the birth pains, apostasy, abomination, persecution). The generation that is alive to see these events take place will "know that it is near."

Therefore, not knowing the "day and hour" is once again proven to be in general because "this generation" will not pass away until all these things have happened.

And once again, the coming/rapture is not a thief to us if we are prophecy-understanding believers. As we will find out after this study is completed, "this generation" that sees all these things will be the generation that also sees Christ's return!

Jesus continues to tell us in verses 45–47 that because we don't know at what time the master is coming, we should obey. Christ just exhorts us to be prepared, keep watch, be faithful, and not lose heart because we want to be living a life that pleases Him when He does come. Once again, He never states that we won't know what will happen first or what is coming soon. He has repeatedly made it clear that we will know He is right at the door because of the signs.

How High Is the Sky Anyway?

The proponents of the pre-trib doctrine claim that the entire passage we've just looked at can't be referring to the rapture for a number of reasons, most of which we have seen. One of their main lines of reasoning is that, in verse 31, it says that His angels will "gather His elect from the four winds, from one end of the *heavens* to the other." They say that at the time Matt. 24:31 is fulfilled, we will have been in heaven for at least seven years because of the rapture. Therefore, this gathering in Matthew 24 must be God gathering us, the Church, together from heaven and returning with us at the end of the Tribulation for the battle of Armageddon. They come to this conclusion partly because the verse says that we will be gathered "from one end of the *heavens* to the other."

First of all, as you recall from the earlier pages, the whole thought of us returning with Christ to battle at Armageddon is completely unfounded. Scripture states no such thing. Secondly, just because the word "heavens" is used doesn't mean the matter is closed. The word "heavens," as seen here in Matthew, is *ouranos* (Strong's 3772) in its original Greek form, which can mean the literal heaven where God resides, or it can simply mean the whole expanse of the sky where the birds fly and the rain forms (Matt. 6:26, James 5:18). This should show us that we shouldn't be too quick to jump to conclusions about this passage referring to us returning with Christ from heaven. The realm of heaven where Christ is seated next to the Father is in sharp contrast to the sky we see above, and within the context of Matthew 24, *ouranos* is clearly speaking of the "sky" we see above as it is translated in the NASB, not heaven where God resides.

> And He will send forth His angels with a great trumpet and they will gather together His elect from the four winds, from one end of the sky to the other .(Matt. 24:31, NASB)

While no chapter tells us everything, if we put all of the end-times passages found in all of the books of the Bible together and lay them on top of each other, the holes fill in so that we have a complete and orderly picture. As we've seen, Luke adds information that Matthew doesn't, as does 1 and 2 Thessalonians, Revelation, and many other books.

While Matthew only says that we will be gathered from one end of the heavens (sky), Mark adds:

> And he will send His angels and gather His elect
> from the four winds, from the ends of the *earth* to
> the ends of the heavens. (Mark 13:27)

The reference to "the earth" in Mark now fills the hole Matthew left vacant and the problem is solved. At the sounding of the trumpet, those who are dead in Christ will be raised first (1 Thess. 4:16), and then those of us who are still alive will be "caught up" from the earth to the sky and the angels will gather us together also (1 Thess. 4:17). It is actually pretty simple. Followers of Christ, dead and alive, will be gathered from everywhere, from the ends of the earth to the ends of the sky to be with our Lord forever.

Dictionary Dilemma

We have now concluded Matthew 24, but before we begin in 1 Thessalonians, I feel the need to expound on a few things.

I have discussed the pre-tribulation doctrine of imminence several times. Pre-trib teachers tell us that Christ's return is imminent, saying that He could come at any moment and that nothing has to happen first. As I'm sure you have seen by now, I disagree with this teaching. I believe pre-trib teachers have taken great liberty with the Bible and made all sorts of assumptions.

I do believe that Christ's return is imminent, however—just not in the way the teachers tell me.

IMMINENT = Likely to happen soon, about to occur, overhanging.

The term "imminent" in no way means nothing has to happen first. As H. L. Nigro has pointed out, there are many instances in which events are considered to be imminent and yet things must happen before they occur, including the rapture. Although Nigro gives different examples, I'll insert my own here: My wife thinks I'm the greatest man on the planet (sometimes) when she isn't mad at me for not picking my dirty clothes up off the floor. When I've been out of town working for a few days, she wants me to come back. She knows my return is imminent and eagerly awaits it. She is looking forward to it. This doesn't mean that nothing has to happen before my *parousia* (coming) to *paralambano* (receive near) my beautiful bride. I have to finish my work, check out from the Super 8, refill the gas tank, and drive home while listening to my employee complain about his ex-wife.

"Imminent" simply means something is impending. Pre-trib teachers have even manipulated the dictionary.

Christ's return is imminent, *if* the word imminent is used correctly. It will happen soon. We've seen the gospel spreading to almost every nation, and the increase of earthquakes, famines, wars, and rumors of wars. Although I don't believe the true birth pains have begun, it is as if we can almost hear Christ packing His gear as we see the pre-birth pains happening around us. His coming is imminent and may happen in our lifetimes, so let's be ready, living a life of obedience and expectancy.

I hope you are at least beginning to doubt the pre-tribulation theory by now. To find out more, let's look at another "thief" verse in 1 Thessalonians.

4

1 Thessalonians: Another 'Thief'

> According to the Lord's own word, we tell you that we who are still alive, who are left till the *coming* of the Lord, will certainly not precede those who have fallen asleep. For the Lord Himself will come down from heaven, with a loud command, with the voice of the archangel and with the trumpet call of God, and the dead in Christ will rise first. After that, *we who are still alive and are left will be caught up together with them in the clouds to meet the Lord in the air.* And so we will be with the Lord forever. (1 Thess. 4:15–17)

In 1 Thess. 4:13–5:11, Paul goes into detail about the coming (*parousia*) of the Lord. Verses 15–17 tell us in great detail what the rapture will be like. Just as Jesus said in Matthew 24 concerning His coming, there is a trumpet sounded. Then the dead in Christ will be raised. After that, we will be "caught up" together with them to meet the Lord in the air to be with Him forever. Make sure you notice that this happens at the coming (v. 15).

Now 1 Thessalonians 5 begins. Although it is a new chapter, Paul continues the same thought about Christ's coming:

Now brothers, about times and dates [about

which Paul was just talking in 4:13–18] we do
not need to write to you, for you know very well
that the Day of the Lord will come like a thief in
the night. (1 Thess. 5:1–2)

Here Paul ties the rapture/coming with the Day of the
Lord. He does this by continuing on from the rapture
teaching in 4:13–18 to explain that the Thessalonians
don't need to discuss dates concerning the rapture/com-
ing, for they know very well that the Day of the Lord will
come like a thief in the night.

The Day of the Lord comes as a thief? Wait a minute, I
thought the "thief" was referring to when we will be raptured at the coming (remember Matt. 24:43?), not the
Day of the Lord! It is clearly referring to both. Here, Paul
ties the coming, rapture, and Day of the Lord into each
other again. Tying these three things together is very
important. We already connected them in Matthew, and
now we've connected them again in the writings of Paul.
Don't forget it. We will discuss its importance soon.

Paul then continues in verse 3, speaking of the
destruction that will take place during the Day of the
Lord. He then writes:

But you, brothers, are not in darkness so that this
day [the coming/rapture and the Day of the Lord]
should surprise you like a thief. (1 Thess. 5:4)

Once again, Christ comes as a thief to those who are
living in darkness—not to us, just as Jesus said in

Matthew 24. Paul also tells us to be alert and self-controlled, living as sons of the light, putting on faith, hope, and love (v. 5–8), just as Jesus told us to obey in Matt. 24:45–47 so that we are not caught off-guard when He comes. And just like Jesus, Paul ties in the …well, by now you know the three things by heart.

Now verse 9, the other key verse the pre-tribulation doctrine uses:

> For God did not appoint us to suffer wrath but to
> receive salvation through our Lord Jesus Christ.
> (1 Thess. 5:9)

As I said earlier, there's not one verse in the entire Bible that says the entire seven years (Daniel's 70th Week) is God's wrath. Plus, we have just seen that, no, we aren't destined for wrath because we will be "caught up" and delivered from the wrath to come. More on the wrath issue later when we study 2 Thessalonians and tie Revelation into what Jesus and Paul taught.

But for now, notice that this teaching of Paul begins in 4:13 speaking about the rapture at the coming/*parousia* and concludes in 5:10–11, speaking also of the rapture at the coming/*parousia*.

> He died for us so that, whether we are *awake or*
> *asleep* [just as in 4:16–17, whether we are dead or
> alive], we may live together with Him. Therefore
> encourage one another and build each other up,
> just as in fact you are doing. (1 Thess. 5:10–11)

Paul starts and finishes his teaching on the Second Coming by telling us what will happen at the coming/*parousia* of Christ. We will live together with Him! Because this passage begins and ends with the same thought, we can conclude that everything in between is also referring to this thought, which is the rapture at His coming. Once again, the rapture at Christ's coming is not a separate event from the Day of the Lord as the pre-tribulation doctrine would have us believe.

The Last Trumpet

> At that time the sign of the Son of Man will appear in the sky, and all the nations of the earth will mourn. They will see the Son of Man coming on the clouds of the sky, with power and great glory. And He will send his angels *with a loud trumpet call*, and they will gather His elect from the four winds, from one end of the heavens to the other. (Matt. 24:30–31)

> For the Lord Himself will come down from heaven, with a loud command, with the voice of the archangel and with *the trumpet call of God*, and the dead in Christ will rise first. After that, we who are still alive and are left will be caught up together with them in the clouds to meet the Lord in the air. And so we will be with the Lord forever. (1 Thess. 4:16-17)

In Matthew 24, we saw that God will send His angels with a loud trumpet call. Now, in 1 Thessalonians, we've seen the same trumpet, called "the trumpet call of God." We won't be studying the entire passage, but there is a verse within 1 Corinthians that adds even more detail to the trumpet blown by God before He gathers us together at the rapture.

> Listen, I tell you a mystery: We will not all sleep, but we will all be changed—in a flash, in the twinkling of an eye, *at the last trumpet.* For the trumpet will sound, the dead will be raised imperishable, and the mortal with immortality. (1 Cor. 15:51-52)

The pre-tribulation doctrine teaches that Rev. 4:1 records the last trumpet call at the rapture. In reality, this verse simply tells us that John was in the Spirit when he saw the vision recorded in Revelation. Pre-trib teachers hold to the view that this is symbolic of the rapture, and because Jesus' voice sounded like a trumpet, it must be the last trumpet. This is an assumption based on no biblical proof. We will see more about this when we investigate Revelation.

So what is the last trumpet? Many believe it is the seventh trumpet in Rev. 11:15 because it truly is the last trumpet in the book of Revelation. While this is a very good conclusion, I don't think it is the case because the seventh trumpet is blown by an angel, and as you just read in 1 Corinthians and 1 Thessalonians, the "last trumpet" is "the trumpet call of God." This, along with the fact that all of the scriptural evidence points to the rapture as occurring after the sixth seal, is why I don't think the seventh trumpet is the one blown initiating the rapture.

Lessons From Maccabees

We'll come back to this issue in a moment, but for now I want to show you something even more astounding that I believe has everything to do with the last trumpet call of God at the rapture. I want to show you what I believe to be the first trumpet.

If you read Dan. 8:9–14, 23–27, and Dan. 11:21–35, you will see the prophecy of Antiochus IV Epiphanes, a man who would later come in the second century B.C. and cause great distress to the people of Israel. As you will also see, he is a foreshadow of the Antichrist to come in the future during Daniel's 70th week.

The words contained in 1 Maccabees, a book that is found in the Apocrypha,[22] aren't inspired like the words in the Bible, but they are considered to be an accurate historical record. The history of the man prophesied about in Daniel, Antiochus IV, is recorded in the book of 1 Maccabees and gives eerie insight into the fact that his-

---

[22] Apocrypha selections taken from *The Holy Bible: Containing Old and New Testaments with Marginal References and Readings*, printed by the John E. Potter and Company, Philadelphia,1873.

tory will be repeated, but on a much larger scale. Consider these passages from 1 Maccabees 1:

> 10 And there came out of them a wicked root, Antiochus surnamed Epiphanes, son of Antiochus the king, who had been an hostage at Rome, and he reigned in the hundred and thirty and seventh year of the kingdom of the Greeks.

Fact: Antiochus IV gave himself the name Antiochus "Theos Epiphanes," which means Antiochus "the visible god." The future Antichrist will also claim to be God (2 Thess. 2:4).

> 11 In those days went there out of Israel wicked men, who persuaded many, saying, "Let us go and make a covenant with the heathen that are round about us: for since we departed from them we have had much sorrow."

Fact: Antiochus Epiphanes made a covenant of peace with Israel and then broke the covenant, just as the future Antichrist will do (Dan. 9:27).

> 16 Now when the kingdom was established before Antiochus, he thought to reign over Egypt, that he might have the dominion of two realms....
>
> 19 Thus they got the strong cities in the land of Egypt, and he took the spoils thereof.

65

Fact: Antiochus IV attacked Egypt. So will the Antichrist (Dan. 11:42-43).

> 21 And entered proudly into the sanctuary, and took away the golden altar, and the candlestick of light, and all the vessels thereof...

Fact: The Antichrist will exalt himself proudly in the rebuilt temple (2 Thess. 2:4).

> 25 Therefore there was great mourning in Israel, in every place where they were...30 And [he] spake peaceable words unto them, but all was deceit: for when they had given him credence, he fell suddenly upon the city, and smote it very sore, and destroyed much people of Israel...

Fact: There will, of course, be great mourning in Israel again when the Antichrist breaks his covenant with them (this will be shown in Chapter 6). This covenant will also contain "peaceable words."

> 54 Now the fifteenth day of the month Casleu, in the hundred forty and fifth year, they set up the abomination of desolation upon the altar, and builded idol altars throughout the cities of Juda on every side...57 And whoever was found with any the book of the testament, or if any consented to the law, the king's commandment was, that they should put him to death...59 Now the

five and twentieth day of the month they did sacrifice upon the idol altar, which was upon the
altar of God.

Fact: Daniel 11:28 tells us Antiochus IV abolished the
daily sacrifices of the Jews. Daniel 9:27 shows us that the
future Antichrist will do the same (the daily sacrifices
will presumably be re-instituted).

Fact: According to historical record, Antiochus IV
erected a statue of Zeus with the likeness of his own face
on it and made people bow to it or die. Antiochus IV
claimed to be God and sacrificed a pig on the altar within
God's temple (the first abomination) to Zeus/himself and
killed those who refused to worship him.

The future Antichrist will set himself up in the temple,
which will be rebuilt, and claim to be God (the second
abomination), demand our worship, and kill those who
refuse. Like Antiochus, the Antichrist will also have an
idol made in his image for us to bow to or die (Rev.
13:14-15). This is irony at its worst.

64 And there was very great wrath upon Israel.

The destruction of Antiochus Epiphanes is partially
recorded in 1 Macc. 3:16–24 and 4:6–16. The amazing
truth of all of this is that the destruction of Antiochus,
this foreshadowing Antichrist, is not only foretold in
Daniel, but in Zechariah

I will bend Judah as I bend my bow and fill it with Ephraim. I will rouse your sons, O Zion [the Maccabees], against your sons, O Greece [the Seleucids of Syria/Antiochus IV], and make you like a warrior's sword. Then the Lord will appear over them; his arrow will flash like lightning. *The Sovereign lord will sound the trumpet*; he will march in the storms of the south, and Lord Almighty will shield them. They will destroy and overcome with slingstones. They will drink and roar as with wine; they will be full like a bowl used for sprinkling the corners of the altar. The Lord their God will save them on that day as the flock of his people. They will sparkle in his land like jewels in a crown. (Zech. 9:13-16)

Identifying the First Trumpet

Notice my italics in Zech. 9:14. I believe Robert Van Kampen had it right when he wrote that this is the *first trumpet*.[23] Think about it. Antiochus Epiphanes, a man who did almost exactly what the future Antichrist will do, had his army and power destroyed by an army empowered by God when *He blew a trumpet* (Antiochus IV died of illness shortly thereafter—just as the Antichrist will perish shortly after his allotted reign).

After the sign in the sun, moon, and stars, we are told

---

[23] *The Sign*, Robert Van Kampen, Crossway Books, Third Revised Edition, 2000, p. 151.

to lift up our heads because our redemption is drawing near. After this, when God sounds the *last trumpet*, He will come and we will be raptured (Matt. 24:29-31). Then His wrath will begin to destroy the Antichrist and his kingdom, just as it happened in the second century B.C. to Antiochus IV. Now that's irony at its best!

5

2 Thessalonians: The 'Day'

Now let's look at what Paul has to say about the rapture in 2 Thessalonians:

> God is just: *He will pay back trouble to those who trouble you and give relief to you who are troubled,* and to us as well. This will happen *when the Lord Jesus is revealed from heaven in blazing fire with His powerful angels.* He will punish those who do not know God and do not obey the gospel of our Lord Jesus. *They will be punished with everlasting destruction* and shut out from the presence of the Lord and from the majesty of His power *on the day He comes to be glorified in His people* and to be marveled at among all those who have believed. This includes you, because you believed our testimony to you. (2 Thess. 1:6–10)

Notice my addition of the italicized lettering and read through these verses again. This time, only read the italicized sections to simplify the passage down to its meat. Notice that Paul states that God will pay back trouble and give relief when Jesus is revealed. Wrath and relief are given at the same time, just as Jesus said it would be when He correlated His return with the days of Noah and Lot. Paul then says they will be punished *on the day* Jesus comes to be glorified in all who have believed, to make it even more specific. Once again, it is just as Jesus said concerning the coming/rapture/wrath parallel with Noah and Lot. Paul then continues in verses 11–12, telling the Thessalonian church he is praying in hopes of their worthiness so that God will be glorified.

To be sure the statement made in verses 9–10 is truly speaking of Christ's coming/*parousia*, let's look at the rest of Paul's comments. He continues:

> Concerning the [1] coming of our Lord Jesus Christ and [2] our being gathered to him, we ask you, brothers, not to become easily unsettled or alarmed by some prophecy, report or letter supposed to have come from us, saying that [3] the day of the Lord has already come. (2 Thess. 2:1)

Notice that I've divided this passage into three parts. Just as we've discovered in Matthew 24 and 1 Thessalonians, we see once again that (1) Jesus' coming, (2) the rapture, and (3) the Day of the Lord/wrath are tied into each other as being all part of the same event.

We even see another, clarified detail here. The relief (1:7)/rapture (2:1) will take place just before (because we truly aren't destined for wrath—1 Thess. 5:9) but on the same day as the destruction (1:9)/Day of the Lord (2:2). We already looked at this relationship in Matthew, and you may be tired of it by now, but this is very important. We spoke earlier of the Noah and Lot correlation and its deliverance/wrath tie-in, and of its eye-opening "thief" meaning, but we didn't cover the "on the same

71

day" issue. I wanted to save it for this discussion we are now having in 2 Thessalonians.

> It was the same in the days of Lot. People were eating and drinking, buying and selling, planting and building. But *the day* Lot left Sodom, fire and sulfur rained down from heaven and destroyed them all. It will be just like this *on the day* the Son of Man is revealed. (Luke 17:28–30)

> For in the days before the flood, people were eating and drinking, marrying and giving in marriage, *up to the day* Noah entered the ark, and they knew nothing about what would happen until the flood came and took them all away. That is how it will be at the coming of the Son of Man. (Matt. 24:38–39)

> Just as it was in the days of Noah, so also will it be in the days of the Son of Man. People were eating, drinking, marrying and being given in marriage, *up to the day* Noah entered the ark. Then the flood came and destroyed them all. (Luke 17:26–28)

Just to make sure it happened this way and that these verses really are saying that deliverance and wrath were given on the same day (and will be on the same day at Christ's coming), let's look at the original account:

> In the six hundredth year of Noah's life, on the seventeenth day of the second month—*on that*

72

> *day* all the springs of the great deep burst forth,
> and the floodgates of the heavens were opened.
> And rain fell on the earth forty days and forty
> nights. *On that very same day* Noah and his sons,
> Shem, Ham, and Japeth, together with his wife
> and the wives of his three sons, entered the ark.
> (Gen. 7:11–13)

Everything lines up perfectly. Both Jesus and Paul are
telling us that at Christ's coming, He will rapture/gather
the elect/Church, and then—on the same day—pour out
His wrath (beginning of the Day of the Lord).

Why am I making such a big deal about this? Hold on.
We will see very soon.

> Don't let anyone deceive you in any way, *for that
> day* will not come until the rebellion [apostasy:
> see NASB or KJV] occurs and the man of lawless-
> ness is revealed, the man doomed to destruction.
> He will oppose and exalt himself over everything
> that is called God or is worshiped, so that he sets
> himself up in God's temple, proclaiming himself
> to be God. (2 Thess. 2:3–4)

Don't be deceived! "That day" (the Day of the Lord we
have been talking so much about) won't come until the
apostasy occurs and the Antichrist exalts himself, setting
himself up in God's temple, saying he is God. In other
words, the Antichrist *must* commit the "abomination that
causes desolation" *before* the day that Christ comes to
gather His elect and the Day of the Lord begins. As you

probably recall, this also lines up with the teaching of Jesus in Matthew 24 (see chart on page 76).

Many think it is taking the Bible too literally to use the verses found in Matthew 24 and 2 Thessalonians as an "on the same day" reference. Many say that we shouldn't be this literal because it is dangerous.

First of all, I don't feel that I am being liberal in my conclusions. Secondly, I don't believe it is dangerous to take the Bible literally. It is dangerous to *not* take it literally. Of course, there are many passages that are not to be taken literally in every sense, such as parables. Hyperbole is another example, as when Jesus tells us to gouge out our eye or cut off our hand if it causes us to sin (Matt. 5:29–30). This is an obvious exaggeration to show the severity of sin and the seriousness of avoiding it. Likewise, the phrase "in that day" is used more than once in the Bible and is another example of a day being determined by the context. When "in that day" is used, it is speaking of a time period and not a specific day, and is in no way the same as "on the day."

There are also many verses that use the word "as" or "like" to connect two subjects in a simile. A good example of this is as follows:

> But do not forget this one thing, dear friends: With the Lord a day is *like* a thousand years, and a thousand years are *like* a day. The Lord is not slow to keep his promise…. (2 Peter 3:8)

This verse is not saying that a thousand years to us is

a literal day to God. It is just telling us that we are finite and God is infinite, and we cannot understand what slowness truly is because God is outside of time and space. If you look at this passage in its entirety, you'll find it also has to do with the promise of the return of Christ.

We have already seen what I believe to be substantial proof that we will not be raptured until after the persecution associated with the Antichrist when he commits the abomination that causes desolation, which is his act of exalting himself in God's temple, claiming to be God. Which, by the way, happens in the middle of Daniel's 70th Week (Dan. 9:27).

As if all we've looked at isn't enough, we have more.

The Lord Alone Exalted

Now, finally, I will tell you why I've been making such a hoopla about the coming, rapture, and beginning of the Day of the Lord being on the same day. Isaiah tells us about the Day of the Lord:

> The eyes of the arrogant man will be humbled
> and the pride of men brought low; the Lord alone
> will be exalted in that day. (Isaiah 2:11)

The Lord *alone* will be exalted in that day! What does this prove? Once again, it proves the pre-tribulation theory wrong and the Bible right. For if the coming, rapture, and beginning of the Day of the Lord are tied together on the same day, and if this day is before the Tribulation (as the pre-tribulation position contends), how can the Antichrist exalt himself in God's temple 3 1/2 years later? If the entire seven years of Daniel's 70th week is God's wrath in the Day of the Lord, and "the Lord alone will be exalted in that day," how can the Antichrist exalt himself in the middle of it? He can't! It is biblically impossible for the rapture to take place before "the man of lawlessness...exalt[s] himself over everything that is called God or is worshiped, so that he sets himself up in God's temple, proclaiming himself to be God." Don't let anyone deceive you in any way.

Comparison of Matthew 24 and 1,2 Thessalonians		
Matt. 24:4–8	**Birth pains**	
Matt. 24:15	**Abomination that Causes Desolation**	2 Thess. 2:4
Matt. 24:10–12	**Apostasy**	2 Thess. 2:3
Matt. 24:29	**Sign in Sun, Moon, Stars**	
Matt. 24:31, 40–41	**Gathering/Rapture**	1 Thess. 4:15–17, 2 Thess. 2:1
Matt. 24:37–41	**The Coming Initiates Wrath**	1 Thess. 5:1–3, 2 Thess. 1:6–7, 9–10, 2 Thess. 2:1–2

6

Daniel: The 70th Week

We will not go into a deep discussion of all the end-times events spoken of in the book of Daniel. I'm trying to keep this study to the basics so as to not have a huge book. However, there are a few things we should discuss.

First, we see in Dan. 9:20–23 that Gabriel comes to Daniel to deliver a message in the form of a vision while Daniel is praying. Then, we read in verses 24–26 about the first 69 of 70 weeks (also called "sevens") that are decreed for the nation of Israel:

> Seventy "sevens" are decreed for your people and your holy city to finish transgression, to put an end to sin, to atone for wickedness, to bring in everlasting righteousness, to seal up vision and prophecy and to anoint the most holy. (Dan. 9:24)

> Know and understand this: From the issuing of the decree to restore and rebuild Jerusalem until the Anointed One, the ruler, comes, there will be seven "sevens," and sixty-two "sevens." It will be rebuilt with streets and a trench, but in times of trouble. After the sixty-two "sevens," the Anointed One will be cut off and will have nothing (Dan. 9:25–26)

Some translations of the Bible will use the term "weeks" instead of "sevens." A "week" (NASB), or a "seven" (NIV), is a period of seven years. From the time the decree is issued to rebuild Jerusalem (after the Babylonian captivity), we are told that there will be seven and 62 weeks (for a total of 69 weeks) until "Messiah the Prince" (NASB), or the "Anointed One," (NIV) comes.

The first seven "weeks" began with the decree to rebuild Jerusalem and concluded when the rebuilding was completed 49 years later. Remember, there are seven years in each week, so this first period of seven weeks equaled 49 years. Seven (weeks) times seven (years) = 49 years. This is how long the rebuilding of Jerusalem took.

Verse 26 tells us that from the completion of the first seven weeks, there would be 62 more weeks until the Messiah would be cut off to have nothing (or killed, fulfilled in Christ's crucifixion). When we figure all these weeks by multiplication, we see it was 483 years from the issuing of the decree to rebuild Jerusalem until the Messiah would come and be "cut off." Sixty-nine (weeks) times seven (years) = 483 years. Four hundred and eighty-three years after the decree to rebuild Jerusalem is the time that Jesus was crucified around A.D. 32.

When Jesus was crucified, or cut off to have nothing, the 69-week clock was also cut off. The final 70th Week will resume when the ruler who is to come (the Antichrist) makes a covenant with Israel for seven years (one week), as we shall soon see.

When Israel rejected Christ at the cross in unbelief,

the clock stopped. The people of Israel were broken off from the vine (if they were unbelieving) and God revealed His Kingdom to the gentiles and began grafting them into the vine of spiritual Israel (Romans 11:25). He did this to make unbelieving Israel envious (Romans 11:11), so as to turn their faces toward His Son.

Verse 26 tells us even more.

> The people [the people of ancient Rome] of the ruler who will come [the Antichrist] will destroy the city and the sanctuary. The end [of Jerusalem] will come like a flood: War will continue until the end, and desolations have been decreed. (Dan. 9:26)

Notice that the first part of this prophecy has already been fulfilled. Jerusalem was destroyed in A.D. 70 by Titus and the Roman Empire. But this prophecy has two parts. It also refers to a "ruler who will come," the Antichrist, about whom we learn more in verse 27.

> He will confirm a covenant with many for one "seven." In the middle of the "seven" he will put an end to sacrifice and offering. And on a wing of the temple he will set up an abomination that causes desolation, until the end that is decreed is poured out on him. (Dan. 9:27)

Verse 27 explains that he (the Antichrist) will make and then break a covenant with Israel in the middle of the final week and set up an abomination that causes desola-

79

tion. The middle of this week (seven) is three-and-one-half-years. This is when the Great Tribulation will begin. This abomination, described in Dan. 9:27 is the very same abomination that Jesus spoke of in Matthew 24:

> So when you see standing in the holy place "the abomination that causes desolation," spoken of through the prophet Daniel....(Matt. 24:15)

Remember, Daniel was just told that the Antichrist will break the covenant in the middle of the 70th Week, or after three-and-one-half-years. Since each "week" is seven years, this leaves the Antichrist in power another three-and-one-half-years *after* he breaks the covenant.

In Rev. 13:5, we see verification that the time the Antichrist will have authority will be 42 months, or three-and-one-half-years. According to the Jewish calendar, there are 30 days in a month. Therefore, there are 1,260 days of the Antichrist's authority. Forty-two months times 30 (days) = 1,260. This matches up with the three-and-one half years in Daniel. Please read all of Revelation 13 now to have a better understanding of what he will do in this time.

Now we know that the 70th Week will begin at the signing of the seven-year covenant with Israel. Three-and-one half years into that seven years, the Antichrist will break the covenant and set up the abomination that causes desolation. He will claim to be as God and make the world bow to his image. Those who refuse to worship him or take his mark will be killed if they don't escape and hide. Now we have a better understanding of what Jesus was talking about in Matt. 24:15:

> So when you see standing in the holy place "the abomination that causes desolation," spoken of by the prophet Daniel...then let those who are in Judea flee to the mountains. Let no one on the roof of his house go down to take anything out of the house. Let no one in the field go back to get his cloak.

Let's jump over to Daniel 11 for more information about the Antichrist. The end of verse 36 tells us:

> He [the Antichrist] will be successful until the time of wrath is complete. (Dan. 11:36—NIV)

> ...he shall prosper till the indignation be accomplished.... (Dan. 11:36—KJV)

This verse is speaking of Satan's wrath through the Antichrist, not God's wrath on unbelieving mankind. The Hebrew word that has been translated "wrath" and "indignation" is *za'am* (Strong's 2194, 2195). *Za'am*: "froth at the mouth, defy, abominable, fury, be angry, indignation, rage (esp. of God's displeasure with sin)." The discussions we had earlier about the final seven years of Daniel's 70th Week and its entirety not being God's wrath is seen in part here. We see in verse 36 that much

Daniel's 70 Week Timeline

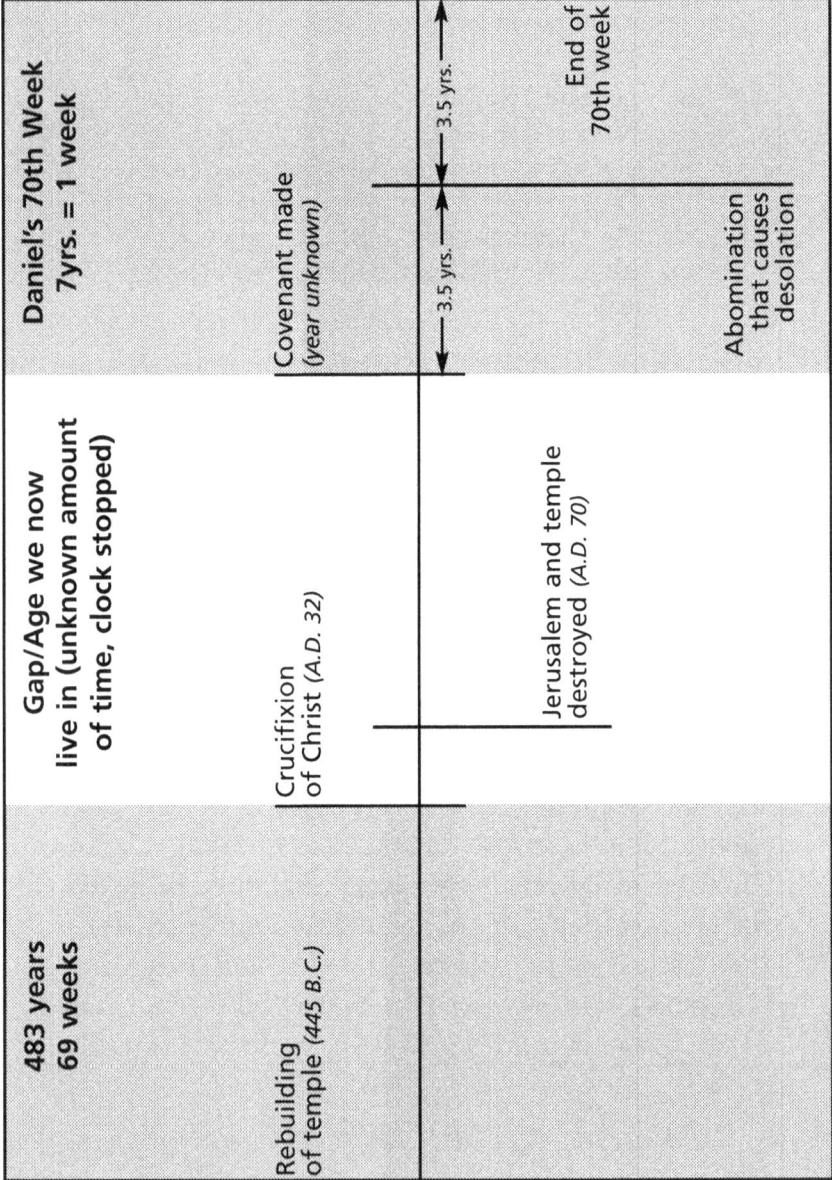

**483 years
69 weeks**

Gap/Age we now live in (unknown amount of time, clock stopped)

Daniel's 70th Week
7yrs. = 1 week

Rebuilding of temple *(445 B.C.)*

Crucifixion of Christ *(A.D. 32)*

Jerusalem and temple destroyed *(A.D. 70)*

Covenant made *(year unknown)*

3.5 yrs.

3.5 yrs.

End of 70th week

Abomination that causes desolation

of the last "week" will be Satan's wrath on man (because of his hatred of God's displeasure with sin), through the Antichrist, not God's wrath on Satan and the ungodly.

Whose People?

Once again, just as they've done with Matthew 24, pre-trib teachers tell us that this prophecy has nothing to do with us because Dan. 9:24 says, "Seventy 'sevens' are decreed for *your people* (Daniel's people)." Because it says "your people," the illogical conclusion is made that it must be for Daniel's people *only*. Keep in mind that nowhere in scripture does it say, "The end-time suffering is only for Israel," but this is the leap pre-tribulation teachers have taken.

How often was the Church mentioned in the Old Testament? Never. The Church was a mystery that wasn't fully revealed until after the time of Christ. Therefore, it lacks common sense to conclude that passages such as Dan. 9:24 are only applicable to Israel simply because of the words "your people."

The most logical parallel to this discussion I've found to date comes from a conversation I had with H. L. Nigro. Nigro's view is:

> If the weatherman tells me that it will rain in my town tomorrow, this does not mean that it will not rain in the neighboring town unless he specifically says that the weather pattern will be

restricted to my local area. Likewise, if the scriptures tell us that the 70th Week is applicable to Israel, this does not mean that it is *not* applicable to the Church unless the scriptures specifically tell us so. They do not. There is nothing in the scriptures that tells us that the events of the 70th Week are exclusive to Israel.

Another example is the Ten Commandments. Who were they written to? There is no debate that they were given to Israel. The introduction to the first commandment even says,

> I am the Lord your God, who brought you out of Egypt, out of the land of slavery. (Gen. 20:2)

Christians today weren't in Egyp,t and we have certainly never been their slaves. Does this mean the Ten Commandments are not for us, but only for Israel? Of course not. God never stated that the Ten Commandments were exclusively for Israel. Plus, we know from the New Testament that they apply to us as well, just as we've been seeing throughout this study that the end-times persecution and Daniel's 70th Week are for us, also.

This prophecy in Daniel amazes me. Four-hundred-plus years after the decree to rebuild Jerusalem was the time to begin looking for the Messiah. These verses in Daniel should have made it clear to the Jews living at that time that the Messiah was coming in their lifetimes. They had the calendar right in front of them and still they rejected Jesus! Many understood the prophecies of Daniel and were looking for the Messiah, but those who didn't study the scriptures and listened to men had no idea that Jesus had to be the Anointed One. What a great example of why we need to search the Bible for truth rather than listening to those around us!

This is also a great example for us concerning His return. If the timing of Christ's First Coming was so readily available for the Jews through scripture, why wouldn't the timing of His Second Coming be attainable, too? No, we cannot know when the 70th Week will begin, but when it *does* begin with the ruler's (the Antichrist's) covenant with Israel, we, like ancient Israel at Christ's First Coming, will also have a calendar. We will be able to approximate when Christ will return for us within a few years.

I am not setting dates. We cannot know when the 70th Week will begin, when the rapture will occur, or whether we are the generation that will see Christ's return. Maybe the covenant is being made as you read this and maybe it will happen in two thousand years. But I believe that these things we are studying should be searched through and understood by all followers of Christ. With dedication, it is not impossible. The things we are looking at are the very basics of Second Coming prophecy and should be the bare minimum of our knowledge on this subject. We don't want to make the same mistakes the Jewish nation made.

7

Revelation: The End and a New Beginning

Yes, I'm one of those nuts who believes Revelation is one of the most amazing books in the Bible. Genesis begins the written journey into God's heart and mind, and Revelation completes it. Genesis introduces us to the history of creation, while Revelation foretells its end.

Revelation is overflowing with truths that apply to us in our everyday walks with God. Our desperate need for God, His guidance, and an obedient, persevering heart that yearns for a life led by the Spirit penetrate the chapters from beginning to end. The spiritual realm of good and evil that surrounds us is painted across every page with great detail that forces us to ponder. So many topics of truth are included within its pages, including Israel, the Church, the different strengths and weaknesses within the professing church, a long-suffering but just God, grace, wrath, sovereignty, Satan and his followers, and a never-ending love that God has given to all who know His Son, to name just a few.

I believe Revelation is filled with things that are symbolic, but I also think there are many things to be taken literally. Deciphering between the two, and seeking the meaning of the symbolism, takes a careful consideration of the entire Bible.

In doing this, I have concluded that The Revelation of Jesus Christ is just that, the revealing of Jesus, His ways, His thoughts, His heart, and much, much more. I am also convinced that this book reveals future events in a step-by-step order that lines up with Daniel, Matthew, 1 and 2 Thessalonians, and the many other books that contain promises and prophecies throughout the Bible.

The things I find continually stimulate me to know and understand Jesus and His ways more completely every time I search this book. There are so many things I have yet to discover, and many things I don't think I'll ever understand until I meet Him, but I don't plan to abandon the search.

I hope the few pages ahead motivate you to seek His face and His plan more thoroughly, for Rev. 1:3 tells us:

> Blessed is the one who reads the words of this prophecy, and blessed are those who hear it and take to heart what is written in it, because the time is near. (Rev. 1:3)

'I Will Keep You From the Hour of Trial'

Now let's take a look at one of the most controversial verses in the rapture debate: "I will keep you from the hour of trial" (Rev. 3:10).

Remember my comment in the introduction? That this is the only verse in the entire Bible that even appears to say we will not go through the Tribulation? This is the verse pre-trib teachers use as the foundation for the entire theory. Yes, at first glance, it seems to tell us that we will be kept from the persecution, but I believe this verse has been slaughtered by the pre-trib doctrine and needs to be investigated.

We've been told what this verse means by pre-trib teachers so many times that it is hard to see it any way other than what they tell us it means. I hate to start off with such a confusing verse, but I feel that it is very important not to skip over this pre-trib foundation.

So far, everything we've looked at in Matthew and 1 and 2 Thessalonians has said the opposite of what Rev. 3:10 appears to be saying, so it would be unwise to throw out everything we've seen thus far because of one verse. Please study this on your own, with *Strong's Concordance* and a Bible with a Greek parallel and dictionary, so that you have more than just my word.

The seven churches in the beginning of Revelation each receive a letter coming from the mouth of Jesus. Each letter addresses that church's present state, as well as a future promise, both of which are relevant to us in this lifetime. The promises given to these churches are based on the same principle as the promises given to men like Abraham in Hebrews 11, meaning that they didn't get to see them fulfilled in their lifetimes, but they will be fulfilled in the future.

This is the promise given to the church of Philadelphia that is causing all of the controversy:

Since you have kept my command to endure patiently, I will also keep you from the hour of trial that is going to come upon the whole world to test those who live on the earth. (Rev. 3:10 NIV)

Because you have kept the word of My perseverance, I will also keep you from the hour of testing, that hour which is about to come upon the whole world, to test those who dwell upon the earth. (Rev. 3:10— NASB)

Because thou hast kept the word of my patience, I also will keep thee from the hour of temptation, which shall come upon all the world, to try them that dwell upon the earth. (Rev. 3:10—KJV)

Defining 'Keep'

As we begin our study of this verse, let's start with the phrase "I will keep you." The word "keep" in its original language is *tereo* (Strong's 5083). *Tereo* means to watch over protectively, or to guard. I believe the use of the word *tereo* in Rev. 3:10 is speaking of the keeping of our/the church of Philadelphia's soul, or the keeping of us spiritually. "Kept by God" is a good way to look at it.

Tereo is translated "preserved" in Jude and 1 Thessalonians, and I believe this word best explains the way it is used in Rev. 3:10. We are kept or preserved in Christ because He is the One who holds our salvation.

Jude, the servant of Jesus Christ, and brother of James, to them that are sanctified by God the Father, and preserved [*tereo*] in Jesus Christ, and called. (Jude 1:1—KJV)

Now may the God of peace Himself sanctify you entirely; and may your spirit and soul and body be preserved [*tereo*] complete, without blame at the coming of our Lord Jesus Christ. (1 Thess. 5:23—NASB)

Defining 'From'

Next, let's look at the word "from." *Ek* (Strong's 1537) is what has been translated "from" in this passage. *Ek* in the *Strong's Dictionary* is defined as "a state or condition, out of which one comes."

What is the "state or condition" that Rev. 3:10 is speaking of? The condition is the hour of testing (NASB), hour of trial (NIV), or hour of temptation (KJV) that is going to come upon the whole world. When *ek* is combined with *tereo*, as it is in Rev. 3:10—*tereo ek*—it forms the meaning of being watched protectively, guarded, or preserved, out from within the midst of the hour of temptation, the condition believers will be in.

If we were to be kept away from the hour of temptation—as in removed by the rapture, as pre-trib teachers would have us believe—instead of *ek*, *apo* (Greek) would have been used. *Apo* (Strong's 575) means "away from" or to "separate from something." In John H. Dobson's book, *Learn New Testament Greek*,[24] there is an illustration showing two people standing in a house and then walking out of it to show the meaning of *ek*. As an example of *apo*, two people are shown walking away from the house to clarify the difference between the two words.

I feel the statement, "I will keep thee from the hour of temptation" is better understood in English to mean: "I will spiritually keep you, out from within the midst of the temptation."

Here is a good example. While Jesus is praying to His Father in the book of John, He says:

> I do not ask Thee to take them out of [*ek*] the world but to keep [*tereo*] them from [*ek*] the evil one. (John 17:15—NASB)

Jesus isn't asking for us to be taken out from within the midst (*ek*) of the world. He is asking for the Father to spiritually preserve (*tereo*) us out from within the midst (*ek*) of the evil one. We are not kept away from (*apo*) the world and Satan in distance. We are preserved while in the world and within the midst of Satan's evil and influence. *Tereo ek* is combined here as it is in Rev. 3:10.

Now let's take a peek at what LaHaye has to say about this verse. I think it is quite interesting. LaHaye gives these verses as examples to prove that *ek* means we will

---

[24] *Learn New Testament Greek*, John H. Dobson, Baker Book House, 1989, p. 72.

be kept out of, or away from, the Tribulation.[25]

> *"Out of* Egypt I have called My Son." (Matt. 2:15)

> "First cast out the beam *out of* thine own eye. (Matt. 7:5)

> "...for *out of* the heart proceed evil thoughts." (Matt. 15:19)

> "And [many bodies of saints] came *out of* the graves after His resurrection." (Matt. 27:53)

> "I will spew thee *out of* My mouth." (Rev. 3:16)

Do you see it? Every one of these verses translate *ek* to say "out of." Every one of these verses speaks of something coming out from within the midst of something else, not being kept away from something completely! Each one of these verses could also be translated "from": from Egypt, from thy own eye, from the heart, from the graves and from My mouth.

Interesting, very interesting.

---

[25] *Rapture Under Attack*, p. 50.

What Kind of Temptation Is It?

It seems to me that the meaning of keep/*tereo* and from/*ek* have both been interpreted by men with pre-conceived ideas. But I also believe the "hour of trial," (NIV)/"testing," (NASB)/"temptation" (KJV) has quite possibly been missed, in part, by them too. Most have concluded that "the hour of temptation" is referring to the physical time period of the Tribulation and what goes on within that period. I think it is deeper than that.

> Because thou has kept the word of my patience, I also will keep thee from the hour of *temptation*, which shall come upon all the world, to try them that dwell upon the earth. (Rev. 3:10 KJV)

"Temptation" has been translated from *peirasmos* (Strong's, 3986), which comes from *peirazo* (Strong's, 3985), which means "to try," to prove in a good sense or a bad one.

> Blessed is a man who perseveres under trial [*peirasmos*]; for once he has been approved, he will receive the crown of life, which the Lord has promised to those who love Him. (James 1:12—NASB)

This shows us that one of the purposes of temptation (*peirasmos*) is to approve us. We will be blessed if we persevere (i.e. "keep the word of [His] perseverance" as it says in Rev. 3:10—NASB) until His coming.

We know that God does not tempt (James 1:13), but He does allow Satan to tempt us. He allows tempting as a test, to prove our hearts genuine or false. What God said to Satan in the first chapter of Job is a good example: "Have you considered My servant Job?" (Job 1:8). Satan was allowed by God to take away Job's children, wealth, and property. This was a physical test, and was only part of the larger test. The larger test was an inward, spiritual test to prove Job's righteousness by his willingness or refusal to succumb to the temptation to deny God. Likewise, 1 Peter 4:17 tells us that judgment begins with the house of God. This "test" during Daniel's 70th Week is, in part, a purification process to divide the true followers from the false.

Who Will Be 'Kept'?

I think of the temptation in Rev. 3:10 as being like Job's temptation. It is not just the physical time period of the temptation itself. It is the spiritual act of being inwardly tempted by Satan to deny God and worship the Antichrist during the Great Tribulation. Those who have kept Christ's command to persevere, as Job did, will be rescued out from within the temptation to deny Him as Job was. Job's faith in God, his perseverance and understanding of God's sovereignty, helped him to refuse the temptation and stand strong in the belief that God is always right. It will be the same for those of us who persevere in the way that the church of Philadelphia did. Notice the verse right before Rev. 3:10:

> I know that you have little strength, yet you have kept My word and have not denied My name. (Rev. 3:8)

I think that those of us who have persevered, kept His Word, and not denied His name will be spiritually rescued from the temptation to deny His name during the temptation the rest of the Church will be facing.

> Because He Himself suffered when He was tempted, He is able to help those who are being tempted. (Heb. 2:18)

If you read about the other six churches spoken of in Revelation, you will see that five of them are warned to repent of their half-hearted ways. If they don't, Christ promised serious consequences such as, "I am about to spit you out of my mouth" (Rev. 3:16). These five churches are doing what many of us call "walking the fence" in this day and age. These "fence walkers" who enter the Tribulation are in danger of the serious consequences that will come as a result of failing the test during the persecution of the Antichrist.

Now that we have looked at all this, I feel Rev. 3:10 is really saying, "Because you have kept My command to persevere, I will spiritually keep you and deliver you out from within the midst of the hour of temptation that is going to come upon the whole world as a test to prove who is truly Mine."

There is also another possible, very simple interpretation for this passage. What if the test that the Church will be kept from is the Day of The Lord? The Day of the Lord begins at, or immediately after, the rapture. The phrase, "those who dwell on the earth (NASB)," is found 10 other times in Revelation, and each time it is referring to those who are hostile to God. Though I lean towards my first conclusion, I see the possibility that this verse could be saying, "Since you have kept my command to endure patiently, I will also keep you from the Day of the Lord that is going to come upon the whole world to test My enemies." Whatever the case may be, Rev. 3:10 does not say, "Pre-trib rapture."

Not Fit for a Foundation

All pre-trib teachers use 3:10 as a rapture verse. In *Are We Living in the End Times?* LaHaye speaks of this verse, saying, "The guarantee of rapture before Tribulation could hardly be more powerful. No wonder one writer labeled it 'a cardinal Scripture.'"[26]

Now that we've examined Rev. 3:10, it should be obvious that this verse is very complicated and should not be a foundation for anything. It bears absolutely no "pow-

---

[26] *Are We Living in the End Times?*, p. 109.

erful" qualities that support the pre-tribulation theory. I will humorously agree that it is a "cardinal Scripture" for the pre-tribulation theory, though.

I believe Rev. 3:10 is of spiritual content from beginning to end. Those who have *spiritually* persevered will be *spiritually* preserved and *spiritually* delivered out from within the midst of the *spiritual* temptation (to deny Christ), which is allowed by God as a spiritual test for the world. I know the Bible is wholly inspired by God, but this does not mean that every word that men have translated or interpreted from the original texts is inspired. We need to study deeply for ourselves so as to not be fooled by men's interpretations or by tricky translations.

This is certainly not the last word on Rev. 3:10, and I encourage you to dig in and study all this carefully for yourself.

Now, let's continue the study.

Unrolling the Scroll

Chapter 5 begins with the introduction of a scroll sealed with seven seals, which only Christ can open. The seven seals placed on the scroll are the same seven seals we will investigate further in Revelation 6–8.

As each seal is removed, a particular event transpires. Once all seven seals are removed, then and only then can the scroll be opened. As I will attempt to prove, I believe the scroll contains God's wrath, which will not be unleashed until the scroll is opened (see chart on p. 100). This, of course, will prove that we do not need to be raptured before the Tribulation as the pre-trib theory claims. If God's wrath upon man doesn't begin until the trumpet judgments, we do not need to be raptured before the Tribulation.

Also, I will show ample proof that the seals are Satan's wrath upon man rather than God's wrath upon man, which of course, once again proves that we don't need to be raptured before the Tribulation. We are promised only that we will be saved from the wrath of God. God has never promised that we will be saved from the wrath or persecution of Satan.

As we will see, this lines up with everything we've considered thus far. If I am right, the words Jesus spoke in Matthew 24 will line up with the things He showed John in Revelation.

The Seals

Revelation 6:1 begins the opening of the first seal. This is where many readers' problems begin. I know, because I saw the seals as the wrath of God at one time, too. It looked so obvious. Christ opens a seal and bad things happen. God's wrath, plain and simple. I no longer see it this way.

Just because Christ opens a seal and bad things happen doesn't mean that it is His wrath. Everything in this world falls under God's sovereignty. He either does something or allows something to be done. He is the one in control—not us, not fate, and certainly not Satan. Just like the wrath upon Job was Satan's wrath and not God's, but allowed by God, the opening of the seals are God's sovereign allowance of events to transpire and His allowance of Satan's wrath upon man.

Let me compare the life of Job with a recent event we can all relate to. Vern Kuenzi, author of *Restoring the Vision of the End-Times Church*, recently commented on his Web site about the terrorist strike on the World Trade Center. Kuenzi states:

> …we are under His increasing judgment. However, these judgments are redemptive in nature. The Bible says that when God pours out His judgments, the people learn righteousness. May it be so. The Bible also indicates that there is a suffering for righteousness' sake and a suffering because of sin. What of this are we to know in the lives of those who perished [on September 11]? Only God knows. The Bible says God disciplines those He loves. Ultimately, whether this [the World Trade Center bombing] is a suffering for sin or for righteousness' sake, it is a discipline or judgment designed in part to conform us who are left alive to His likeness because He loves us. Remember also that Job

Seals Opened in Revelation 6

God's wrath is contained inside the scroll. Only when all seals are removed can the scroll be opened to reveal His wrath.

FIRST SEAL
Conqueror bent on conquest

SECOND SEAL
Peace taken from the earth

THIRD SEAL
Famine

FOURTH SEAL
Death

FIFTH SEAL
Martyred saints

SIXTH SEAL
Sun, moon and stars sign

SEVENTH SEAL
Opens the scroll containing trumpet and bowl judgments

was a righteous man, but God allowed Satan to collapse the house on all of Job's children.[27]

Some don't think a good God would allow such a thing. While I don't necessarily agree that the bombing was God's judgment, He did allow it to occur. The Bible is clear that God does allow, and even ordains, trials and afflictions in our lives to test and refine us. I'm hoping that because you have actually made it this far into the study you probably have a fair grasp of sovereignty, so I won't discuss this issue. Here are a few verses on which you may meditate, however, if you are wondering what all this sovereignty talk is about: Gen. 25:23; Joshua 11:20; 1 Sam. 2:6–8; 1 Kings 18:1; 1 Chron. 29:11; John 6:37, 39, 44; Romans 9; and Eph. 1:3–14.

Remember all that we looked at in Matthew 24? The birth pains, apostasy, abomination, sign in the sun, moon, and stars, and the rapture and wrath all fit into the 70th Week of Daniel, which also fit into Revelation. It seems as though we may now be feeling pre-birth pains, but I believe that the true birth pains about which Jesus taught will occur when the seals of Revelation are opened.

---

[27] http://www.restoringthevision.com/wtc.htm

The First Seal

Now look at the first seal (Rev. 6:1–2):

> I watched as the Lamb opened the first of the seven seals. Then I heard one of the four living creatures say in a voice like thunder, "Come!" I looked, and there before me was a white horse! Its rider held a bow, and he was given a crown, and he rode out as a conqueror bent on conquest.

Notice that one of the four living creatures says "Come!" and the event happens. Nothing is mentioned about God doing anything or pouring out wrath in any way. The only way we could say that this is God's wrath is by assumption.

We then see a conquering rider with a bow, sitting on a white horse, and he is given a crown. It seems that this rider is the Antichrist. It fits the order of the things to come and what we have looked at in our study so far. The Antichrist *is* a conqueror and the crown may represent his rule of the earth.

In Matt. 24:5, Jesus told us that many false christs will come and deceive many. We know from the book of Daniel that the covenant the Antichrist will make with Israel will kick off Daniel's 70th Week, which is what a big portion of Revelation is all about. Therefore, it is only fitting that when the first seal is opened, the Antichrist's covenant and plans begin to unfold.

102

The Second Seal

> When the Lamb opened the second seal, I heard
> the second living creature say, "Come!" Then
> another horse came out, a fiery red one. Its rider
> was given power to take peace from the earth and
> to make men slay each other. To him was given a
> large sword. (Rev. 6:3–4)

Once again, a living creature says "Come!" and this
time a rider on a red horse is given power to take peace
from the earth. This lines up with what Jesus said in
Matt. 24:6–7 concerning wars and rumors of wars and
nation against nation. It is interesting to note that this
does not *have* to be God's wrath, even though pre-tribulation teachers tell us it is. Here, we see men against men,
which *usually* fits under the realm of Satan and his influence rather than God's.

The Third Seal

> When the Lamb opened the third seal, I heard
> the third living creature say, "Come!" I looked,
> and there before me was a black horse! Its rider
> was holding a pair of scales in his hand. Then I
> heard what sounded like a voice among the four
> living creatures, saying, "A quart of wheat for a
> day's wages, and three quarts of barley for a day's
> wages, and do not damage the oil and the wine!"
> (Rev. 6:5–6)

"A quart of wheat for a day's wages, and three quarts of barley for a day's wages, and do not damage the oil and the wine!" represents famine and lines up with the famine in Matt. 24:7. It is assumed that famine has to be God's wrath, but this does not have to be true. For just as fire fell from the sky, destroying Job's sheep and servants, and wind destroyed Job's house and family, this famine is just as natural as what Satan did to Job using weather. Satan has more power than we tend to give him credit for.

The Fourth Seal

> When the Lamb opened the fourth seal, I heard the voice of the fourth living creature say, "Come!" I looked, and there before me was a pale horse! Its rider was named Death, and Hades was following close behind him. They were given power over a fourth of the earth to kill by sword, famine and plague, and by the wild beasts of the earth. (Rev. 6:7–8)

The angel says, "Come!" and we now see a pale horse with a rider named Death. Hades is following close behind. They are given power over one-fourth of the earth to kill by sword, famine, plague, and by the wild beasts of the earth.

Robert Van Kampen has made a suggestion in his books *The Sign* and *The Rapture Question Answered: Plain and Simple* concerning the word "beasts" (*therion*, Strong's 2342) in verse 8. Although this word can simply mean "beasts," as in animals, *therion* is used 38 times in the book of Revelation. Other than verse 8, every time *therion* is used, it is used to refer to *the* beast or beasts, which would be the Antichrist and his false prophet. Van Kampen suggests that the wild beasts of the earth in verse 8 are none other than the Antichrist and his false prophet. I feel this is certainly a possibility.[28]

Chapter 13 of Revelation gives a big picture view of the times of the Antichrist. In Rev. 13:7, we see that he is given power to make war with the saints and overcome them. This also lines up with Jesus' teaching. If Van Kampen is right with his "beasts" theory, the fourth seal may represent the midpoint of the 70th Week where the Antichrist sets himself up to be God. This would make sense, considering that the fourth seal is followed by the death of the martyrs (see below), and the midpoint of the 70th Week is followed by the Great Tribulation. Once again, the timing is perfect.

Although perfect timing is not the central theme of this book, such things are interesting to me. The main point I've been trying to make, and the theme I've been pursuing, is that the rapture will not take place until after the persecution during the Great Tribulation.

---

[28] *The Sign*, Robert Van Kampen, p. 267; *The Rapture Question Answered: Plain & Simple*, pp. 147-149.

The Fifth Seal

Remember, the pre-trib doctrine tells us that the entire 70th Week—the seals, trumpets, and bowls—are God's wrath. If nothing I've said so far has been convincing, I hope the fifth seal should tie the knot, showing that the seals cannot be God's wrath.

> When he opened the fifth seal, I saw under the altar the souls of those who had been slain because of the word of God and the testimony they had maintained. They called out in a loud voice, "How long, Sovereign Lord, holy and true, until you judge the inhabitants of the earth and avenge our blood?" Then each of them was given a white robe, and they were told to wait a little longer, until the number of their fellow servants and brothers who were to be killed as they had been was completed. (Rev. 6:9–11)

If the proponents of the pre-tribulation doctrine stick with their belief that each time a seal is opened another step in God's wrath is taken, they must admit that, in the fifth seal, God is killing His own saints. When the fifth seal is opened, could God be the one killing His followers? This makes no sense.

An even bigger problem arises when this passage is investigated a little deeper. In Rev. 6:10, the martyred saints cry, "How long, O Lord, holy and true, will You refrain from judging and avenging our blood on those who dwell on the earth?" If God's wrath has been poured out since the opening of the first seal, wouldn't He already be judging those who dwell on the earth and avenging the martyrs' blood? But, because of this passage, we clearly see that He is not judging nor avenging, and therefore is not yet pouring out end-times wrath as the pre-tribulation doctrine claims.

This being so, the statement, "The Bible clearly teaches that we aren't destined for God's wrath, so we must be raptured before the Tribulation" doesn't pass the test. There are no verses that say the seals are God's wrath, and the only "proof" the pre-trib teachers have of the rapture occurring before the seals is Rev. 3:10, which is no proof at all.

Another "proof" pre-trib teachers often appeal to is Rev. 4:1:

> After this I looked, and there before me was a door standing open in heaven. And the voice I had first heard speaking to me like a trumpet said, "Come up here, and I will show you what must take place after this."

LaHaye and most other pre-trib teachers claim that the command, "Come up here," is symbolic of the rapture.[29] Ironically, in page 206 of *Rapture Under Attack*, LaHaye writes, "Spiritualizing the Scripture, even the prophetic passages, can be very dangerous, for it opens the door to private interpretation. In other words, you

---

[29] *Revelation Illustrated and Made Plain*, pp. 75-76.

can conclude almost *anything* with the text." This important rule is precisely the rule LaHaye, himself, is breaking here. The phrase "Come up here" doesn't parallel the rapture by any means. John was not physically caught up to heaven, as we will be when Christ gathers us at His Coming. John was caught up in the spirit, as he clearly states in Rev. 4:2: "At once I was in the Spirit...." The only reason to conclude that this event represents the rapture is if one needs to find a rapture before the Great Tribulation to fit a certain belief system.

Furthermore, if this "Come up here" proves a pre-tribulational rapture, why doesn't the death and resurrection of the two witnesses prove that we will go through the Antichrist's persecution?

> Then they [the two witnesses] heard a loud voice from heaven saying to them, "Come up here." And they went up to heaven in a cloud, while their enemies looked on. (Rev. 11:12)

This takes place well after the Antichrist has begun his persecution and would better serve as a symbolic representation of the rapture because the two witnesses are literally *and* physically transported to heaven in front of the onlookers. But because I do my best to avoid symbolism for proof and search for literalness instead, I reject both of these "Come up here" statements as being the rapture.

Let's return to the fifth seal.

The death of the servants of God in the fifth seal certainly lines up with what Jesus said in Matthew 24 about the Great Tribulation. Whether the fourth or the fifth seal represents the midpoint of Daniel's 70th Week is not absolutely clear. Actually, I don't even feel it is important.

This seal shows us that the killing of those who refuse to bow to the Antichrist has already begun. Because of this, it is also clear that the Antichrist has already set himself up to be God, which takes place three-and-one-half years after the signing of the covenant.

Whose Wrath?

Before we move on to the sixth seal, I want to address the "wrath" issue one more time.

> Since we have now been justified by his blood, how much more shall we be saved from God's wrath through Him! (Romans 5:9)

By this verse, we know that we will escape God's wrath, but we should also know that there is not a single verse in the Bible that says we will never experience *Satan's* wrath—past, present, or future. It would be absurd to believe such a thing. From Genesis to Revelation, God's people have been suffering because of Satan and his desire to devour us. And don't forget, this is always allowed by God, just as we've seen that God allows Satan to persecute us during the Great Tribulation. God is always in control.

In *Rapture Under Attack*, LaHaye states, "God has

promised at least four times that He will save Christians from the wrath to come. It's difficult to conceive of the Tribulation period as anything but a catastrophic time of wrath, for it is described as such at least 10 times (Rev. 6:10; 7:14; 8:13; 11:10, 18; 12:12; 13:7–8, 12, 14; 14:6; 17:2, 8)."[30]

Let's investigate. Verses 6:10; 7:14; 12:12; 13:7–8, 12, and 14 are all referring to Satan's wrath or the effects of it. Here are just two examples:

> Therefore rejoice, you heavens and you who dwell in them! But woe to the earth and the sea, because the devil has gone down to you! He is filled with fury [wrath—NASB], because he knows that his time is short. (Rev. 12:12)

> He was given power to make war against the saints and to conquer them. And he was given authority over every tribe, people, language, and nation. All inhabitants of the earth will worship the beast—all whose names have not been written in the book of life belonging to the Lamb that was slain from the creation of the world. (Rev. 13:7–8)

LaHaye has just told us that a portion of the 70th Week is Satan's wrath! This is exactly the point *I've* been making. The seals are not God's wrath, and every verse cited by LaHaye proves it. They are Satan's wrath. The

---

[30] *Rapture Under Attack*, p. 201.

passages shown above, from chapters 12 and 13, are detailed pictures of the seals. The other passages (Rev. 8:13; 11:10, 18; 14:6; 17:2, 8), which *are* examples of God's wrath, are verses that show events that take place *after* the seals. Are you getting this?!

The Sixth Seal

The sign of the sun, moon, and stars we saw in Matthew has arrived! In Matthew, Jesus taught that the Church would be raptured after this sign. If Jesus said those things in Matthew and also showed these things to John, they should line up shouldn't they? Indeed, they do.

> I watched as he opened the sixth seal. There was a great earthquake. The sun turned black like sackcloth made of goat hair, the whole moon turned blood red, and the stars in the sky fell to earth, as late figs drop from a fig tree when shaken by a strong wind. (Rev. 6:12–13)

The pre-trib teachers tell us that the sign in the sun, moon, and stars in Rev. 6:12-14 is not the same sign as seen in Matthew 24, but we have seen proof that the signs in Matthew and Revelation are one in the same. There is too much order for them to be different signs. Notice the next passage:

> Then the kings of the earth, the princes, the generals, the rich, the mighty, and every slave and

111

every free man hid in caves and among the rocks
of the mountains. (Rev. 6:15)

Immediately after the triple sign of the sun, moon, and stars, men become fearful and hide in the rocks. This lines up with what Luke tells us will happen after the triple sign, and immediately before Christ returns, in his record, too.

Men will faint from terror, apprehensive of what
is coming on the world. (Luke 21:26)

Isaiah also records the same episode while describing the Day of the Lord:

They will flee to caverns in the rocks and to the
overhanging crags from dread of the Lord and the
splendor of His majesty.... (Isaiah 2:21)

Is it only a coincidence that we have been seeing that the sun will turn black, the moon will turn blood red, and the stars will fall from the sky before Christ returns and the Day of the Lord begins? Is it only a random circumstance that we see men hiding at the same time in many books of the Bible? If I have been correct, we should soon see evidence of the rapture and the beginning of the Day of the Lord.

"For the great day of their wrath has come, and
who can stand?" (Rev. 6:17)

Finally, after the sixth seal has begun, we see the word "wrath" used for the first time. It comes from the mouths of the people seeing the earth-shattering disturbances all around them. Finally, the people of the world believe that God is God and He is filled with wrath.

Remember, this statement, "God's wrath has come," is what John sees men concluding because of the disturbances. It doesn't necessarily mean His wrath has literally arrived, for the scroll has not yet been opened.

I don't want to take any more space on this subject than I have to, but feel free to study the Greek to find that the phrase "has come" is in the present tense and doesn't mean that wrath has been around since the first seal. The King James Version translates this verse as "is come" and better shows what's really being said.

Chapter 7 is a bigger picture of what happens before God's wrath is literally poured out on the inhabitants of the earth. In Rev. 7:1–3, we see four angels holding back the four winds to prevent any wind from harming the earth. This is not solid proof, but it is interesting to note that the four winds are also mentioned in Matt. 24:31, right after the sign in the sun, moon, and stars, as we are being gathered by the angels.

The four winds in Revelation represent God's wrath, which must be held back a little while longer until the 144,000 chosen Jews have seals placed on their foreheads, sealing them in salvation so that they will be saved from the wrath to come.

One More Nail in the Coffin

In Matthew 24 and 1 Thessalonians, we saw that Christ's coming is associated with the rapture and the Day of the Lord. They are not separate events. In 2 Thessalonians, we saw added information to clarify this fact to an even further degree: The rapture and the beginning of the Day of the Lord occur on the same day.

This makes a pre-trib rapture biblically impossible because "the Lord alone will be exalted" during the Day of the Lord (Isaiah 2:11). If the rapture and the beginning of the Day of the Lord are on the same day, as the Bible has indicated, and if the Lord alone will be exalted during that Day, the Antichrist cannot exalt himself three-and-one-half years after a pre-trib rapture when the Day of the Lord is already in effect. As we know, the Antichrist will, in fact, exalt himself at the midpoint of Daniel's 70th Week. This puts the pre-trib rapture in direct conflict with scripture.

Furthermore, in Matthew 24, and now in Revelation, we have seen that many events must take place before the triple sign in the sun, moon, and stars takes place, which is the sign that must take place before the Day of the Lord will begin.

> The sun will be turned to darkness and the moon to blood before the coming of the great and dreadful day of the LORD. (Joel 2:31)

Also, as we have seen, this sign mentioned in Joel 2:31

does not take place until the sixth seal is opened. This biblical fact once again makes the pre-trib rapture impossible. Because we know that the rapture will take place on the same day that the Day of the Lord begins, and because we know that this "Day" will not begin until sometime after the cosmic signs at the sixth seal, we can conclude, once again, that the rapture cannot occur before the first seal as the pre-trib theory claims.

With these facts, we are able to further understand why this day will not surprise us like a thief.

> But you, brothers, are not in darkness so that *this day* should surprise you like a thief. (1 Thess. 5:4)

"This day" will not become reality until after the sixth seal is opened, so we therefore have the preceding seals, the abomination of desolation, and the cosmic signs as signals that warn us of Christ's impending return. This truth completely destroys the pre-tribulation teaching that Christ could return at any moment and that nothing has to happen first.

The Rapture

In Matthew 24 Jesus tells us that we will be "gathered" after the sign of the sun, moon and stars, then God's wrath will come. We have just seen this sign in the sixth seal, and if I've been correct in my conclusions, we

115

should also see evidence of the rapture soon after these same signs in Revelation.

> After this I looked and there before me was a great multitude that no one could count, from every nation, tribe, people and language, standing before the throne and in front of the Lamb. They were wearing white robes and were holding palm branches in their hands. (Rev. 7:9)

> Then one of the elders asked me, "These in white robes—who are they, and where did they come from?" I answered, "Sir, you know." And he said, "These are they who have come out of the great tribulation; they have washed their robes and made them white in the blood of the Lamb." (Rev. 7:13–14)

No, we aren't shown the actual rapture, but we are shown the effects of the rapture. We are shown a great multitude that *came out of* the Great Tribulation right after the sign in the sun, moon, and stars, which certainly fits into the big picture of what Jesus told us in Matthew 24! Look now at an earlier verse in Revelation:

> You [Christ] purchased men for God from every tribe and language and people and nation. (Rev. 5:9)

This is speaking of us. All of us who have been bought by the blood of the Lamb. It is the exact same language used to show the great multitude that "came out" of the Great Tribulation in Rev. 6:9.

Also, in verses 11–12, we see the angels, elders, and four living creatures praising God because of the people who have obtained salvation and have "come out" of the Great Tribulation. If the Church is already here, in heaven, because of a pre-tribulation rapture—as pre-trib teachers claim—why isn't the Church also seen in this passage, greeting these new arrivals? And why are the angels, elders, and living creatures praising God for these people? Because they are the Church, rescued by means of the rapture after the sign in the sun, moon, and stars, just like Jesus said!

> Therefore, they are before the throne of God and serve Him day and night in His temple; and He who sits on the throne will spread His tent over them. Never again will they hunger; never again will they thirst. The sun will not beat upon them, nor any scorching heat. For the Lamb at the center of the throne will be their Shepherd; He will lead them to springs of living water. And God will wipe away every tear from their eyes. (Rev. 7:15–17)

What a beautiful glimpse of what we have to look forward to! He will give us white robes (Rev. 7:9) and make us as pure as the blood of the Lamb, protecting us, wiping away every tear and all pain, and bringing us into eternity (see also chapters 21–22)!

The great multitude that comes out of the Great

Tribulation can be nothing less than those who are still alive to be caught up at the coming of our Lord (1 Thess. 4:17). As I conveyed earlier, if we put the end-times passages found in the other books of the Bible together and lay them on top of each other, the holes fill in so that we have a complete and orderly picture. Once again, we are seeing this firsthand. Everything fits in an orderly fashion within all we've studied in Daniel, Matthew, and 1 and 2 Thessalonians.

The Seventh Seal

Don't forget Joel 2:31, which tells us the sign in the sun, moon, and stars will come *before* the Day of the Lord. We have just seen this sign in the sixth seal, so with this in mind, let's see if God's wrath truly does come after this sign.

In Rev. 8:1, we now see the opening of the seventh seal:

> When he opened the seventh seal, there was silence in heaven for about half an hour. (Rev. 8:1)

Do you remember the scroll? Now that the seventh seal has just been removed, we should see the wrath of God begin because the scroll can now be opened. And we do.

> Then the angel took the censer, filled it with fire from the altar, and hurled it on the earth; and

> there came peals of thunder, rumblings, flashes
> of lightning and an earthquake. (Rev. 8:5)

This hurling is the first act we have seen God (or at least an angel/His agent) take towards those who oppose Him. As one looks at the trumpet and bowl judgments, it becomes clear that God's judgment/wrath has begun.

Conclusion

The things written in the book of Revelation correlate with all we have looked at in Daniel, Matthew, and 1 and 2 Thessalonians. The birth pains Jesus mentioned are seen in Revelation. Both Jesus and Paul said that suffering and the abomination of desolation would take place before the rapture. Revelation said the same. Jesus told us that there would be a sign given in the sky before we are gathered. We've seen that, too. Jesus and Paul just told us the wrath of God will begin immediately after the rapture. And once again, we've seen that in Revelation, too.

And yet, nothing we have looked at contradicts Christ's words when He said:

> Therefore keep watch, because you do not know
> on what day your Lord will come. (Matt. 24:42)

All we know is that, at an unknown time, there will be

a covenant made with Israel and the birth pains will begin. Three-and-a-half years after the covenant is made (of which we may or may not be informed), the Antichrist will set himself up to be God, which will initiate the persecution and killing of those who refuse to take his mark and bow to his image. Sometime between that three-and-one-half year midpoint and the conclusion of Daniel's 70th Week, we will see the sun go dark, the moon turn blood red, and the stars fall from the sky. Then, and only then, will we be raptured.

If we are alive to see these things happen, we will be the generation spoken of in Matthew 24. If we are the generation that sees all of these signs, we will know His return is near. We know "all these things" will take place within Daniel's 70th Week, which is only seven years long, so if we see all these things, we know that we will be the generation to be gathered to our God between the midpoint of the 70th Week and the end.

If we see the sign in the sun, moon, and stars, that's when we are told to lift up our heads because our redemption is drawing near!

Comparison of Revelation 6 & Matthew 24

1st Seal	Rev. 6:1-2	Conqueror Bent on Conquest; Antichrist	**Matt. 24:5**	False Christs; Antichrist	
2nd Seal	Rev. 6:3-4	Peace Taken from Earth	**Matt. 24:6-7**	Wars; Nation Against Nation	
3rd Seal	Rev. 6:5-6	Famine	**Matt. 24:7**	Famine	
4th Seal	Rev. 6:7-8	Sword, Famine, Plague, Beasts	**Matt. 24:15,21**	Great Tribulation (NAS, KJV)	
5th Seal	Rev. 6:9-11	Martyrdom	**Matt. 24:9, 22**	Martyrdom	
6th Seal	Rev. 6:12-14	Sun, Moon and Stars Sign	**Matt. 24:29**	Sun, Moon, and Stars Sign	
	Rev. 7:9-14	Great Multitude Comes out of the Great Tribulation	**Matt. 24:31**	Elect Gathered; Rapture	
7th Seal	Rev. 8:1-6	Scroll Opened; Wrath of God	**Matt. 24:37-39**	Wrath of God	

8

Putting It All Together

If we put all this together, what do we have? Here is a combination of the relevant scripture verses we have looked at so far, along with a few others, in order to get the simplified, big picture. Some of the passages have been paraphrased to help them flow together.

Watch out that no one deceives you.[31] And be on guard, for Christ has told us everything in advance.[32] The Antichrist will confirm a covenant with Israel for seven years.[33] And many will come in Jesus' name, claiming, "I am the Christ," and will deceive many. You will hear of wars and rumors of wars, but see to it that you are not alarmed. Such things must happen, but the end is still to come. Nation will rise against nation, and kingdom against kingdom. There will be famines and earthquakes in various places. All these are the beginning of birth pains.[34]

Then, in the middle of the "week,"[35] when you see the Antichrist standing in God's temple, exalting himself,

---

31 Matt. 24:4

32 Mark 13:23

33 Dan. 9:27

34 Matt. 24:5-8

35 Dan. 9:27

proclaiming to be God[36] and demanding worship,[37] you will be handed over to be persecuted and put to death, and you will be hated by all nations because of Christ.[38]

At that time there will be an apostasy,[39] when many will turn away from the faith and will betray and hate each other, and many false prophets will appear and deceive many people. Because of the increase of wickedness, the love of Christ will grow cold for most, but he who stands firm to the end will be saved. And the gospel of the kingdom will be preached in the whole world as a testimony to all the nations.[40]

If you are in Jerusalem,[41] when you see the Antichrist exalting himself[42] in the middle of the "week,"[43] flee for your life. Let no one on the roof of his house go down to take anything out of the house. Let no one in the field go back to get his cloak. How dreadful it will be in those days for pregnant women and nursing mothers, for there will be great distress unequaled from the beginning of the world until now, and never to be equaled again.[44]

---

[36] 2 Thess. 2:4

[37] Rev. 13:12

[38] Matt. 24:9

[39] 2 Thess. 2:3

[40] Matt. 24:10-14

[41] Matt. 24:16

[42] 2 Thess. 2:4

[43] Dan. 9:27

[44] Matt. 24:16-18, 21

The Antichrist will be successful until the time of his wrath is complete.[45] If those days were not cut short, no one would survive, but for the sake of the elect, those days will be shortened.[46]

Immediately after the distress following the abomination,[47] there will be a great earthquake. The sun will turn black like sackcloth made of goat hair, the whole moon will turn blood red, and the stars in the sky will fall to the earth, as late figs drop from a fig tree when shaken by a strong wind.[48] These are the signs that the Day of the Lord is about to begin.[49]

When you see all these things, stand tall and look up, for you know that your redemption is near, right at the door.[50] For at that time, the sign of the Son of Man will appear in the sky, and all the nations of the earth will mourn. They will see the Son of Man coming on the clouds of the sky, with power and great glory.[51] The trumpet call of God will sound and the dead in Christ will rise first. After that, those of us who are still alive in Him will be caught up together with them in the clouds.[52] The Lord will send His angels and they will

---

[45] Dan. 11:36

[46] Matt. 24:22

[47] Matt. 24:29

[48] Rev. 6:12-13

[49] Joel 2:31

[50] Luke 21:28, Matt. 24:33

[51] Matt. 24:30

[52] 1 Thess. 4:16-17

gather us from the four winds, from one end of the sky to the other.[53]

He will punish those who do not know God and do not obey the gospel of our Lord Jesus. They will be punished with everlasting destruction and shut out from the presence of the Lord and from the majesty of His power on the day He comes to be glorified in His people and to be marveled at among all those who have believed. This includes you, if you believe the testimony.[54]

His return will be the same as it was in the days of Noah. For in the days before the flood, people were eating and drinking, marrying and giving in marriage, up to the day Noah entered the ark, and they knew nothing about what would happen until the flood came and took them all away. That is how it will be at the coming of the Son of Man.[55]

Now brothers, about times and dates we have no need to worry, for you know very well that Christ's return will be like a thief in the night. But you, brothers, are not in darkness so that this day should surprise you like a thief.[56] So, as was mentioned before, be on guard, for Christ has told us everything in advance![57]

---

[53] Matt. 24:31

[54] 2 Thess. 1:7-10

[55] Matt. 24:37-39

[56] 1 Thess. 5:1-2,4

[57] Mark 13:23

Don't let anyone deceive you in any way, for His return will not come until the apostasy occurs and the man of lawlessness is revealed, the man doomed to destruction.[58]

But don't let your heart be troubled.[59] Those who suffer He delivers in their suffering and He speaks to them in their affliction.[60] Trust in the Father and His Son. In the Father's house are many rooms. If it were not so, Jesus would have told us. But it *is* so, and He has prepared a place for us. And if He prepares a place for us, He will come back and take us to be with Him. We know the way to the place He has gone.[61]

So don't forget, He died for us so that, whether we are awake or asleep, we may live together with Him. Therefore, encourage one another and build each other up, just as in fact you are doing.[62] Be confident that He who began a good work in you will carry it on to completion until the day of Christ Jesus.[63] Eagerly wait for Him to be revealed,[64] but be patient until He does come.[65] And prepare your minds for action. Be self-con-

---

[58] 2 Thess. 2:3

[59] John 14:1

[60] Job 36:15

[61] John 14:1-4

[62] 1 Thess. 5:10-11

[63] Phil. 1:6

[64] 1 Cor. 1:7-9

[65] James 5:7

trolled. Set your hope fully on the grace to be given you when Jesus Christ is revealed![66]

Looking at This Visually

Now, let's take a look at some charts that will help bring these points home. First, a timeline that shows what we've seen so far (page 128).

Remember, the "coming" concerning Christ's future Second Coming is always *parousia*, a noun. If it were a verb, the "coming" would be a simple activity of Jesus coming from there to here. The fact that it is a noun makes it a person, place or thing. It is a thing, an event, like Christ's First Coming. As we discussed earlier, He didn't simply come from heaven to earth and that was it. All aspects of his 33-year life were a part of the First Coming. Likewise, the Second Coming spans an unknown time period containing many occurrences. *Parousia* means "to come and stay," or a continuing presence.

So here's how it happens: Christ's *parousia* begins, we are raptured, and then God's wrath begins when the first trumpet is sounded and is completed in the battle of Armageddon. Everything between the rapture and battle is a part of Christ's coming/*parousia*. Once the battle of Armageddon is completed, we will enter the thousand years of Christ's reign.

---

[66] 1 Peter 1:13

Christ's Parousia

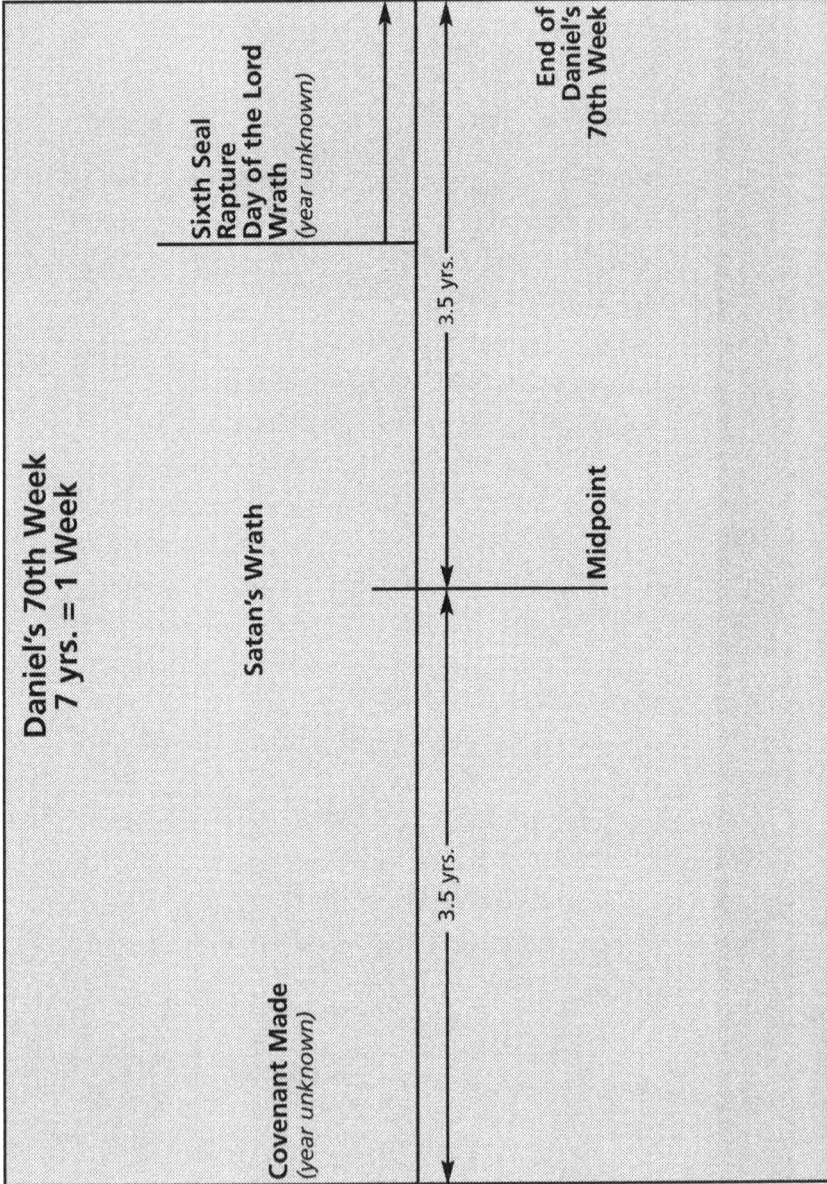

Daniel's 70th Week
7 yrs. = 1 Week

Covenant Made
(year unknown)

Satan's Wrath

Sixth Seal
Rapture
Day of the Lord
Wrath
(year unknown)

Midpoint

End of
Daniel's
70th Week

3.5 yrs.

3.5 yrs.

The Structure of Revelation

The order in which things happen, as recorded in Revelation, has long been debated. The post-tribulation rapture theory, as well as some pre-tribulation theories, teaches that the seals, trumpets, and bowls all take place at the same time. There are too many contradictions in this approach for it to hold water. As just one example, consider the passages in Revelation that state "after these things," which indicate consecutive order rather than events occurring at the same time. This is only one of many reasons.

LaHaye believes that Revelation is consecutive, but still places events in an order to fit a belief system of escaping persecution rather than a logical order. For instance, on page 68 of *Understanding the Last Days*, his chart shows the seals and trumpets covering the first half of Daniel's 70th Week and the bowls covering the entire second half.

Revelation 16 shows in great detail what will happen during the time the bowls are poured out upon the earth. Because of the worldwide disaster taking place as the result of God's wrath, when read literally, it is impossible for this to be a time when the Antichrist is gaining great power and organizing control as he will be doing beginning at the midpoint of the 70th Week. LaHaye's chart also shows that the bowls in Revelation 16 will be poured out during the time period described in Revelation 13, even though nothing hints at this conclusion.

This chart seems to show the most logical order in which the book of Revelation is structured and can be of great help when studying:

Structure of Revelation	
CHAPTERS IN CONSECUTIVE ORDER	
Revelation 1	Introduction to Revelation
Revelation 2-3	Warnings to the Churches
Revelation 6	Account of Seals
Revelation 8-9	Account of Trumpets
Revelation 16	Account of Bowls
Revelation 19	Jesus Rides Forth to Battle
Revelation 20-22	1000 Year Reign / New Heaven and New Earth
HIGHLIGHTS AND PARENTHETICAL VIEWS	
Revelation 4-5	Heaven / Large Scroll
Revelation 7	Deliverance
Revelation 10	Good / Bad News of Future Events
Revelation 11-14	Big Picture of Events During Seals and Trumpets
Revelation 15	Introduction to Bowls
Revelation 17-18	Big Picture of the Harlot / Babylon

9

Will the Antichrist Rule the Whole World?

While I was in my twenties, I worked a gross number of hours and lost a lot of sleep. Life was rough one week, in particular. I even got lost while driving in my own neighborhood because my body was so sleep-deprived! I woke up one morning at about nine o'clock and frantically realized I was late for work. I took a shower, brushed my teeth, grabbed a piece of pizza, and ran out the door.

I had only made about five sprinting steps when I realized that it was pitch black outside. In shock, I stopped as fear began to creep through me. I sat down and began to ask God what was going on. Had the rapture happened and had I been left behind? I was sure the pre-tribulation rapture was wrong, but in my confusion, I had to wonder.

After about ten minutes of sitting on the porch, praying, I decided to turn on the television to see what the news was reporting about this lack of sun in the morning. I wanted to see if there had been airplane crashes or auto crashes around the world because of disappearing people. As I flipped through the channels, I began noticing that every show was an evening show. I was bewildered. Then, I looked at my digital clock, which informed me it was 9 p.m., not 9 a.m. I had fallen asleep a few hours before and simply thought it was morning when I woke up!

More Indoctrinated Than We Think

Why do I tell you this story? It is an example of how indoctrinated we are with pre-trib thought. Even though I had studied the subject and was fully convinced of its error, I was quickly dragged into a pre-trib frame of mind that the rapture could come without even a whisper and that, at any peaceful moment in my day, cars could crash, airplanes could collide, and the end could begin. Yes, I was fairly young, and we could write off this incident as a youthful naiveté, but I've heard of countless stories just like it and am convinced that we would be surprised at just how much the pre-trib theory has affected our thinking, even as mature adults.

Shortly after this book was completed, I was speaking with H. L. Nigro on the telephone and she made the following observation: "What if we have been so indoctrinated with pre-trib philosophy that even those of us who are opposed to the teaching have adopted many of their thoughts without knowing it?" she said.

"Like what?" I responded.

"Like, for example, that the Antichrist will not control the entire world," she explained. "The prophet Daniel said that the Antichrist will rule the 'revived' Roman Empire, so how could the Antichrist control the whole world? The Roman Empire was limited to the Mediterranean region. Therefore, wouldn't the Antichrist's region of direct control be the boundaries of the former Roman Empire? This kinds of shoots down the idea of a 'one-world government' that we've been taught, doesn't it?"

I was surprised. I had never heard anyone make this suggestion before. She proceeded to read a passage to me that I was familiar with, a passage that clearly shows that the Antichrist will not control every nation on earth, but I hadn't thought of it in this way before. Now I was curious, so I decided to check out her theory and get back to her. Now, after studying, I am confident that she has made a valid observation.

Worldwide Domination?

What if we have all been wrong? What if we have all adopted even more end-times hype that will only cause more confusion when the time comes? What if the Antichrist will not control the whole world as we have been told? The idea certainly sells books, but is it biblical? I feel that it is certainly interesting enough to fulfill one of the purposes of this book, which is to make us, the Church, think outside of the box concerning end-times, spiritual matters.

This passage (and a few others) appears to say that the whole world will be ruled by the Antichrist:

> One of the heads of the beast seemed to have had
> a fatal wound, but the fatal wound had been
> healed. The *whole world* was astonished and fol-
> lowed the beast. (Rev. 13:3)

But another passage, which H. L. pointed out to me,
says that Edom, Moab, and the leaders of Ammon *will be
delivered* from the Antichrist's hand:

> At the time of the end the king of the South will
> engage him in battle, and the king of the North
> will storm out against him with chariots and cav-
> alry and a great fleet of ships. He will invade
> many countries and sweep through them like a
> flood. He will also invade the Beautiful Land.
> *Many* countries will fall, *but Edom, Moab and the
> leaders of Ammon will be delivered from his hand.*
> He will extend his power over *many* countries;
> Egypt will not escape. (Dan. 11:40-42)

Though the passage in Revelation tells us that the
whole world will follow the Antichrist, this section of
Daniel tells us that he will only "extend his power over
many countries." How can the Antichrist rule the whole
world but not dominate these three countries? It appears
to be a contradiction. And, if these three countries,
which are very close to Jerusalem, will be delivered from
his hand, it only seems plausible that other countries
that are further away from the Antichrist's seat of power
could avoid falling into his destructive agenda, as well.

After racking my brain on this concept for a while, I decided to search through my concordance for every phrase that contained "the whole earth" or "the whole world," just as it was used in Rev. 13:3 to describe the Antichrist's reign. What I found was very interesting.

'The Whole Earth'

Here are the best examples of passages containing the phrases "whole earth" or "whole world" that, in fact, refer to a local area:

> Babylon was a gold cup in the LORD's hand; she made *the whole earth* drunk. The nations drank her wine; therefore they have now gone mad. (Jer. 51:7)

Did Babylon really make the whole earth "drunk"?

> "I am against you, O destroying mountain [Babylon], you who destroy *the whole earth*," declares the LORD. "I will stretch out my hand against you, roll you off the cliffs, and make you a burned-out mountain." (Jer. 51:25)

Did Babylon destroy the whole earth?

> The *whole world* sought audience with Solomon
> to hear the wisdom God had put in his heart. (1
> Kings 10:24)

The whole world sought Solomon?

> First, I thank my God through Jesus Christ for
> you all, because your faith is being proclaimed
> throughout *the whole world*. (Rom. 1:8, NASB)

Within a few years, the early believers' faith had
reached the whole world?

And another example:

> ...if you continue in your faith, established and
> firm, not moved from the hope held out in the
> gospel. This is the gospel that you heard and that
> has been proclaimed to *every creature under
> heaven*, and of which I, Paul, have become a ser-
> vant. (Col. 1:23)

During the first century, the gospel had been proclaimed to every creature?

I'm sure you're getting my point, but now take note
of these last two examples, which we will look at shortly.
These verses are particularly interesting considering
that, like the "whole world" passage in Revelation, they
have an end-times context. They come from the prophecies of Daniel, which describe the "beast" empires that
will dominate world history until the time of the end.
These examples are referring to previous beasts,

whereas the Antichrist is the final beast (or head of the final beast empire).

> After you, another kingdom will rise, inferior to yours. Next, a third kingdom [Greece], one of bronze, will rule over *the whole earth.* (Dan. 2:39)

Other passages of scripture tell us explicitly that this third kingdom is Greece. Did Greece rule the whole earth? Certainly not.

> He gave me this explanation: "The fourth beast is a fourth kingdom [Rome] that will appear on earth. It will be different from all the other kingdoms and will devour *the whole earth*, trampling it down and crushing it." (Dan. 7:23)

Conservative scholars agree that the fourth kingdom is ancient Rome. Did Rome rule the whole earth? We know for a fact that it didn't.

Conclusions for Us, Today

If all these "whole world" and "whole earth" verses cannot be taken as being literally the whole earth, but rather as being from the perspective of the writer (because, from their perspectives, the entire Mediterranean world was the whole earth), should we jump to conclusions and dogmatically proclaim that the Antichrist will control the whole world? Could it be that the final beast empire will once again be somewhat local and not worldwide, just as all of the other previous beast empires were? Have we been suckered by sensationalism and bought into a modern-day myth?

While I am certainly not suggesting that the final persecution will not involve us, for we should never have an escapist mentality, I feel that the teaching concerning world-wide domination should be questioned. It is just one more of the many things we need to consider because I'm more than confident that we will be in for enough surprises if the end-times events begin in our lifetime. We don't need to add more confusion than there will already be.

10

Does Any of This Really Matter?

I believe this is a very important issue. Every belief either helps or hinders the Christian walk, depending upon its truthfulness or lack thereof. I believe, as I hope you do after reading this book, that the timing of the rapture and Christ's return is as clear as glass. The Great Tribulation must take place first. Many people have told me that great men have debated and disagreed about this topic for years, and if the scholars can't nail down the truth, it must be unsolvable and not important. I believe this is not an accurate way to assess the situation.

Is salvation by grace alone, or is it by works? Can we lose our salvation, or do we have eternal security? Was our inheritance of the kingdom predestined or is it completely up to our choosing? These questions can all be answered with scripture, yet people have been arguing over these issues, I'm sure, since the time of Christ.

Pick any biblical subject and I'm confident you will be able to find books that debate each other vehemently about it. Also, within each disagreement, you will be able to find many followers on each side of the issue. Does this mean that these debates are biblically unsolvable and not important? Of course not. If we believe that the Second Coming issue cannot be solved because of all the opposing views, how can we ever come to a conclusion about anything? Everything is debated.

If this study is correct, and I firmly believe it is, the damaging potentials of the pre-trib doctrine are great. Today, the pre-trib doctrine is more popular than ever because of the amazing sales of the *Left Behind* book series and movie. Almost every time I try to discuss my views with friends, they usually say something like this: "The *Left Behind* series isn't really a 'preacher' of the pre-trib theory. It is just a story of what could happen, and does a great job of showing the non-believer of their need for Jesus. It has been used for good in so many people's lives. What's the harm in this?" The rest of the conversation usually goes okay, but it is also quite obvious that they think I'm making an issue out of nothing until we discuss it further.

The times I've tried to explain to strangers the way I see the matter is a completely different story. The last few years have taught me to keep quiet, unless led otherwise, whenever I am in certain environments. The times I dared to ask questions for people to ponder, the conversation quickly ended. In fact, people usually got mad and sharply told me we are not destined for wrath and that I need to learn to study the Bible. I usually walk away very frustrated, feeling like a complete oddball, wondering why we, as believers, can't openly discuss what we think the Bible says.

So what is the big deal? The pre-trib doctrine is taught as a biblical truth and yes, *Left Behind* is a huge proponent of this doctrine. Listen to the title again: *Left Behind*. The entire series is based on the premise that Christians living before the seven years of Daniel's 70th Week will have no persecution. We will be raptured before the trouble. We will leave behind those who don't know Christ. Only they will face death by the Antichrist if they choose Christ. It is a security blanket for us and a fear motivator for them.

Thomas Ice is the executive director of the PreTrib Research Center in Washington D.C. The Research Center was founded a few years ago by Tim LaHaye and Thomas Ice to research, teach, proclaim, and defend pre-tribulationism. Look for a moment at what Thomas Ice has to say about the people who go against the pre-trib doctrine:

> One of the things that facilitated the Nazi rise to power in Germany earlier this century was their propaganda approach called "The Big Lie." If you told a big enough lie often enough, then the people would come to believe it. This the Nazis did well. This is what anti-pre-tribulationists like John Bray and Dave MacPherson have done over the last 25 years.[67]

I find it very ironic that this is what is being claimed. Isn't it the pre-trib doctrine that is been repeatedly proclaimed from the rooftops? Isn't it the pre-trib doctrine

---

[67] http://www.according2prophecy.org/raptures.html

that's been accepted by many without question because of majority rule in evangelical Christendom?

The *Left Behind* series has been a best-seller in both secular and Christian circles since it first came on the scene. It has even been on the best-seller list of the *New York Times* and *The Wall Street Journal*. Tim LaHaye and the *Left Behind* series were featured in *Time* magazine, which has 23 million subscribers. The other day, I searched on Amazon.com's Web site and found that they are selling 224 books, videos, etc. by Tim LaHaye, most of which are of the *Left Behind* or pre-trib persuasion. The *Left Behind* series has sold over 37 million copies at the date of this writing. The Internet has more pre-trib sites than I care to count. Recently, while I was at a Christian bookstore, I found over 30 pre-trib books on the shelf, while only one little book by a woman named H. L. Nigro sat by its lonesome, holding to a different view. I've seen the pre-trib rapture on the cover of just about every tabloid in the convenience store check-out racks. *Left Behind*, the book, is sold at Wal-Mart, Kmart, Albertsons, and many other nation-wide stores. The *Left Behind* movie came out in February of 2001, and high-ticket sales put a bug in the ear of a shocked Hollywood. The pre-trib rapture has even been portrayed in an episode of the Simpsons!

Christendom is talking and America is listening.

The majority of evangelicals in America have been persuaded to take the *Left Behind* premise of a pre-trib rapture as fact. As I cruise the Internet, searching Web sites and peeking into chat rooms, I see proof of this daily. I've even seen people say that people like me need to read *Left Behind* so that we can understand the Bible! The pre-trib doctrine has escalated to a point where many people "know" it comes from God's word, and anyone who says otherwise is labeled a false teacher. Many good men have lost their financial support or places in ministries because they voiced their dissenting opinions.

If you have concluded that these books are good even though they might be a little off, consider my thoughts on this issue. God uses all things to accomplish His purposes. He uses evil against itself and turns it around for good every day. Does this mean that the original lie, theft, rape, murder, or adultery is okay because it ended up producing good in the long run? Of course not.

If we conclude that the pre-trib theory is a deception, and that this deception in the foundation of the *Left Behind* series is okay because the book/movie has helped people, I think we're kidding ourselves. If we hold to this philosophy, we are also saying it was okay for Judas to sell Jesus out. It was okay for the leaders to listen to the people, free Barabbas, and crucify Jesus. Well, of course it was okay—if they wouldn't have done these things, Jesus wouldn't have died for our sins and risen from the grave. I am being frivolous, but I'm using the same logic used to conclude these books are okay. The end does not justify the means.

I don't believe that the people who see Jesus for the first time while reading this series would go to hell if they hadn't seen the gospel in *Left Behind*. God is sovereign, and Jesus will not lose one of the souls the Father has given Him (John 6:39). God is bigger than that and simply would have used another way to reveal Himself. People's salvation is not solely dependant upon us (John 6:44, 65; Acts 13:48, Romans 9:1–33).

I am very glad people have found Christ in the *Left Behind* book. I find it very satisfying to see God work and accomplish His will. But I can't, in good conscience, tell myself *Left Behind* is good because of it.

I'm not advocating a revolt against *Left Behind*. I'm not suggesting that we get our knickers in a bunch and picket the theaters and Christian bookstores. I am suggesting that we study the Word of God for ourselves rather then listening to what men tell us the Bible says. I'm encouraging you to take a stand for truth and spread it to the ones you think you should.

How This Affects You

Now, why do I say this issue is important, and why is the pre-trib theory damaging? I see two reasons. The daily spiritual life and the future spiritual life are both affected. Let's look first at the daily issue.

Every pre-trib book I've ever read tells me that the pre-trib doctrine promotes holy living. Many books say that any other view causes many to live a life of fear, which drags a person into a life overcome by defeat. In *Rapture*

Under Attack, LaHaye states, "…Christ could come at any moment. When the church loses this anticipation, she tends to become carnal and spiritually dead."[68]

I claim the opposite. I have no doubt that Christ will not come back until after the persecution and the sign in the sun, moon, and stars. This being so, I'm not spiritually dead. I don't believe anyone who knows me would say I'm half-hearted, and I hope this book has had enough heart to show you I'm not. I love God, His Word, His people, and those who don't know Him. I can hardly wait for Christ to return.

Also, what kind of a man was Peter? Anyone can read the gospels and see that Peter was a little slow in the head, but was still whole-hearted from the beginning. As we see later, in 1 and 2 Peter, he became a strong man of God. In John 21:18–19, Jesus told Peter that he would die a martyr's death by crucifixion. Tradition holds that Peter was actually crucified upside-down.

Think about this: Peter knew he was going to be killed. After Jesus ascended, did he believe Jesus was going to return at any moment to rapture him? Of course he didn't. He believed that he would be killed because Jesus said he would. Did he become carnal and spiritually dead? Of course not, because he understood that if we love the Lord, we will obey Him (John 14:15).

Joshua, Moses, Enoch, Elijah, Elisha, Daniel, and all the other godly men of the Old Testament weren't

---

[68] *Rapture Under Attack,* p. 212.

expecting the Messiah to rapture them at any moment and they were able to live the life God requires. The thought that we need to believe in imminence the way the pre-trib doctrine defines it is a man-made thought and has little to do with truth.

I'm not saying that anyone who believes in the pre-trib doctrine is not spiritual. This is only one area of the Christian walk. But I do believe the pre-trib doctrine promotes a small view of God and His ways. I feel it affects many, causing them to have a shallow, escapist mentality in which the thought of God being here for us is elevated over the fact that we are here for Him. We are to be on God's side (Joshua 5:13–14). It takes little spiritual depth to accept the thought that we will avoid the persecution of the Antichrist, and therefore this position produces little growth. In my view, this goes against everything Christ taught concerning the trip down the narrow road.

It is not the easy things in life that produce growth. It is the hard things—the tests and trials—that bring maturity.

> Consider it pure joy, my brothers, whenever you face trials of many kinds, because you know that the testing of your faith develops perseverance. Perseverance must finish its work so that you may be mature and complete, not lacking anything. (James 1:2–3)

> Not only so, but we also rejoice in our sufferings, because we know that suffering produces perse-

verance; perseverance, character; and character, hope. (Romans 5:3–4)

In this you greatly rejoice, though now for a little while you may have had to suffer grief in all kinds of trials. These have come so that your faith—of greater worth than gold, which perishes even though refined by fire—may be proved genuine and may result in praise, glory, and honor when Jesus Christ is revealed. (1 Peter 1:6–7)

But rejoice that you participate in the sufferings of Christ, so that you may be overjoyed when His glory is revealed. (1 Peter 4:13)

For it has been granted to you on behalf of Christ not only to believe on Him, but also to suffer for Him. (Phil. 1:29)

To this you were called, because Christ suffered for you, leaving you an example, that you should follow in His steps. (1 Peter 2:21)

Because He himself suffered when He was tempted, He is able to help those who are being tempted. (Heb. 2:18)

Stretching Ourselves to the Limit

If we hold to the view that we will be part of the persecution, we will be spiritually stretched to the limit. I believe we are told this view in God's Word, not only to prepare us for the coming events, but to prune us of our self-love, which is spiritual suffering in the flesh, to bring us to the point where we truly do want His will in our lives rather than our own desires (John 15:2, Romans 5:3–4, Heb. 12:1–12).

I believe, even though there is great trouble lying in our future, that we are still supposed to eagerly await the day Jesus comes back to bring us to His Father's house. It takes a great love of God for one to want His return and for His will to be accomplished, even if we are to suffer for it to happen. This, I feel, is holy living and true spiritual depth.

The believer with true spiritual understanding longs for Christ's return, no matter what we have to go through to see it. Although we are mere men and want nothing of pain, we are to take off the old self and put on the new, clinging to God's hand in faith, trusting His sovereignty and wanting nothing more than to please Him and to be a part of His plan. If suffering to the point of death is His will, the obedient heart submits and accepts His plan. This is what Jesus did and He is to be our example.

Looking to the Future

And now the future issue. Imagine the pre-trib doctrine being wrong, and I hope this has become very easy for you to imagine by now. Here are a few questions I want you to seriously and prayerfully consider. I believe they are valid questions that very well might be possibilities.

1. If the pre-trib doctrine is false, and I have confidence that it is, how will this belief affect the future when the Antichrist makes a seven-year covenant with Israel?

2. Could some continue in their pre-trib thinking, only to be caught off-guard the day they are told to take the mark, or die from starvation, or be martyred at the hands of the Antichrist? History tells us that many Jewish men and women assumed that the Messiah would come in a particular way. Many of these people continued in their thinking. Look what happened as a result.

3. Might some think the Bible is wrong about the rapture and question whether it is wrong about Jesus, too? Once again, history shows us many Jews concluded Jesus was a fraud because He didn't come the way they thought He would.

4. Could the pre-tribulation teaching play a part in the apostasy spoken of in 2 Thess. 2:3? Matthew 24:10 tells us that "many will turn away from the faith." Verses 12–13 tell us, "Because of the increase of wickedness, the love of most will grow cold, but he who stands firm to the end will be saved" (Matt. 24:12–13).

Because the last half of this verse is referring to believers standing firm, we can also know that the first half is speaking of believers, too. Therefore, "the love [for Christ] of most will grow cold" once the persecution begins. We will see many of the people we love, who we thought loved Christ, fall away from Him and submit to the Antichrist. Will professing followers of God fall away from Him when the test begins because He didn't come back the way they "knew" He would? Once again, many Jews did this also.

5. Will some continue to teach that the 70th Week has not begun because we have not been raptured "like the Bible says"? The experts and teachers of the law continued to teach that the Messiah had not come because He didn't come "like the scriptures said."

6. Some people say that, when the 70th Week begins, people will "wake up" and realize their mistake. I disagree. Why would a few natural circumstances like a peace covenant or more earthquakes wake everybody up from their pre-trib philosophy? Jesus turned water to wine, made the crippled walk, raised Lazarus from the dead, and even rose after being crucified. Many still were unwilling to change their minds.

7. 2 Peter 3:3–4 tells us that scoffers will come in the last days and laugh at us, saying, "Where is this coming He promised? Everything goes on as it has since the beginning of creation." Because of the widespread popularity of the pre-trib teachings, and now with the best-selling *Left Behind* series and movie spreading those beliefs around the world, will people in the last days have all the more reason to say such things? Many know we are expecting to be gone before a seven-year covenant is signed with Israel. They know we are expecting to be gone before a one-world leader arises. One can almost hear them saying, "These things have happened and you are still here. Where is this Jesus you preach so loudly? Where is His coming?" Is this a good reason to take the mark? Is this a good way to prove to oneself that Christ is a hoax and Christians are fools?

8. Why has the pre-trib doctrine only become popular within the last century? It is taught that the pre-trib theory has been around since the beginning. But it has not. The early Church fathers did not teach it, and there is no clear reference to a pre-trib rapture until the 1830's when a man by the name of John Darby began to proclaim it.

9. Are we closer to Christ's return than ever before?

10. Is Satan a genius at deception?

11. Has Satan artfully slipped this belief within the Church during these last days because he knows that many of us listen to men rather than to God?

12. Has Satan done this to bring an unprepared Church

into the Tribulation so that we will either deny Christ or be led to the Antichrist like sheep to the slaughter?

While these questions are based purely on possibilities, many people such as myself agree that they need to be asked.

More Tough Questions

Speaking of tough questions, let me show you a letter I recently e-mailed to one of today's most famous pre-trib advocates who has his own TV show, radio broadcast, Web site, and numerous videos and books. Many pre-trib teachers claim that the Day of the Lord begins at the end of Daniel's 70th Week, which, of course, causes a problem if the Bible is right concerning the rapture and the Day of the Lord being a part of the same event and on the same day. This particular pre-trib teacher, however, holds to the view that the rapture and Day of the Lord *do* begin on the same day. There are holes in this also if one holds the pre-trib belief.

> Thank you for all your hard work. I just have one question. I looked at the FAQ's on your Web site and I'm confused. You mentioned that the Day of the Lord begins one minute after the rapture. I found in Joel 2:31 that the sun will be darkened and the moon turned to blood before the Day of the Lord. It looks like this sign in the sun and moon happens in the sixth seal in Rev 6:12–13. How can this be if we are raptured before the

seals begin? Are the first five seals only a minute long? Please help me understand this.

This is the response I got:

> Thank you for contacting us. We believe that the Bible teaches that the Day of the Lord begins immediately after the Rapture and lasts until the end of the Millennium. The Bible tells us that the renovation of the world by fire happens during the Day of the Lord which we know will not happen until after the Millennium.

Talk about avoiding the question! I then sent this letter:

> Thanks for your quick response but I still don't understand. How does the Day of the Lord begin immediately after the rapture if the Day of the Lord doesn't begin until after the sixth seal? Please help me.

There was no response. I sometimes don't know if I should laugh or cry. Why do we ignore the hard questions? Truth should be high on our agenda and should exceed our desire to be right or our fear of being wrong. In *Rapture Under Attack*, LaHaye writes that he believes anger, jealousy, pride, personal vendettas, and shabby scholarship are what motivate people like me to go against the pre-trib doctrine. I am confident that it is actually a love of God, people, and truth that truly drives a man or woman to take a stand against this teaching. After reading this book and studying your Bible, it is my hope that you will seriously consider taking a stand, too.

If I Can, You Can

I clean windows for a living. Some are 20 stories high and some are in nice little old ladies' houses. Either way, it doesn't take a rocket scientist to accomplish these jobs. I'm small-time. I only have four employees, I never went to college, and I barely sneaked through high school because I had "more important things" to do with my time than study. I have absolutely no biblical training from Dallas Seminary or Moody Bible Institute, and I have never stood at a pulpit and preached. Why do I tell you this and take the chance of this writing losing credibility because of my average, everyday status?

Revelation 5:10 and 1 Peter 2:5, 9 tell us that we are priests. 1 John 2:27 tells us that we don't need anyone to teach us because we have the anointing of the Spirit. Though having pastors and elders is a part of God's plan, we don't need them to do the work that we are called to do as a chosen people, the royal priesthood, a holy nation, and the people of God. With God, we are fully equipped. In John 16:13, Jesus tells us that the Spirit of truth guides us into all truth, and not only that, but the Spirit will tell us of what is yet to come. If I, an insignificant window washer, can dive into the Word and find the things of God, you who are quite possibly smarter than I can certainly do the same. We don't need to be big-time entrepreneurs. We don't need scholars to guide us, and college, seminary, or even high school degrees to understand the scripture. All we need is God and an open, humble heart.

This issue has been gnawing at my gut for five or six years now. One day, I casually told my wife that I was going to do something about it if I ever saw a *Left Behind* book issued for kids. The very next day, an advertisement came in my mailbox. Can you guess what it was for? *Left Behind: The Kids.* Little did I know, the kids' books had already been in stores for over a year! I immediately retreated to my basement, stuck my nose in the Bible, and began typing.

If the pre-trib issue is now gnawing at you as well, and you would like to support the effort I'm making, please tell your friends about this book and where they can get it.

> Have nothing to do with godless myths and old wives' tales; rather, train yourself to be godly....Watch your life and doctrine closely. Persevere in them, because if you do, you will save both yourself and your hearers. (1 Tim. 4:7,16)

> Do your best to present yourself to God as one approved, a workman who does not need to be ashamed and who correctly handles the word of truth. (2 Tim. 2:15)

> For the time will come when men will not put up with sound doctrine. Instead, to suit their own desires, they will gather around them a great number of teachers to say what their itching ears want to hear. (2 Tim. 4:3)

Apply It

The few periods of great pain I've experienced in my life have served me well in my search to understand the practical need to eagerly look forward to Christ's return. When we don't long for His return, we lack an important piece of the puzzle that helps complete the vision of hope that we should all have. When we truly yearn for the day of Christ, our view is focused on heavenly things, not on earthly things, just as we are told to do throughout the Bible.

When I was a teenager, I went through a two- to three-year period of severe emotional pain. All I thought about were my enemies, lack of friends, fear, emptiness, and a vision of my hidden, inner turmoil that I thought would last until the day I died. At night, almost weekly, I would sit on the edge of my bed crying, holding a gun to my head while desperately trying to summon the courage to squeeze the trigger. Although I believed in Jesus to a certain degree, I didn't consider the thought of a better place to fix my eyes upon, and the poor understanding I had of spiritual things almost cost me my life. Fortunately, God had other plans and intervened.

In my mid-twenties, after five or six years of growing in my faith, I experienced a year that was very similar to my teenage years. But this time, as I lay in bed weeping and begging God to either help me or terminate me, God repeatedly reminded me of the perfect grace He had given me in His Son, and I would gain glimpses of the future life I would someday have in His presence. I wanted to be pure. I could barely wait to be sinless, praising Him and singing at His feet. I longed for His return with every ounce of my being and was able to wade through my troubles because I had hope for a better future.

Although these experiences were hard, I know they were nothing in comparison to the suffering I, and we, may go through if the end-times persecution happens in our lifetimes. And I know that the yearning I felt for the return of Christ during my previous pain will be overshadowed by the yearning I will experience if the future persecution begins while I'm still alive.

Think of how it will feel to see friends and family rejecting Christ, choosing instead a quick fix of comfort under the plan of the Antichrist. Consider the loneliness that comes from hiding, much like those who hid from Hitler during the Holocaust. We know that many of us will be killed for our faith, but Rev. 13:10 also informs us that some will be captured and taken into captivity. Envision suffering in a concentration camp of some sort as, once again, people like Corrie Ten Boom suffered during the Holocaust.

The only proper way to endure through a time such as this will be with trust, and by setting our hope completely on Jesus and the grace that will be given to us when He is revealed (1 Peter 1:13). We will need to know beyond a shadow of a doubt that His grace is truly sufficient, and that His power is made perfect in our weakness (2 Cor. 12:9). I am confident that if we see the

70th Week of Daniel, and if we are willing, we will experience His power and perfection, Spirit and voice, and undeniable, insurmountable grace in a way we have never known.

To the best of your ability, imagine how it will be during those times, and picture how much more intense our anticipation for Christ's return will be than it is now. Imagine, after a great suffering that seems to never end, seeing the sun going black, the moon turning blood red, and the stars falling from the sky. The tears will flood down our faces as we look up, knowing that the time is near. What fear of man we have left will depart, and the fear of the Lord will make us whole and be clarified as we await to genuinely and physically, and finally, at any moment, approach the literal throne of grace with confidence. Confidence not because of our strength or good deeds, but because of the finished work upon the cross, where Christ died to pay the price and ransom for our souls for a moment such as this.

The sky will split, opening like a scroll, and the One for whom we have been waiting so long will be seen by all as we meet Him in the sky with a larger-than-life embrace of love. Life as we know it will no longer exist, and will be replaced by perfection in the presence of the One who created us.

What will it be like in this moment? How amazing will the sensation of the overwhelming change of our minds, bodies, and spirits "in the twinkling of an eye" really be? What will it be like to have no more sin or a sidetracking, selfish blur?

At this moment, will we dance in His presence, or, in awe of Him, be still? Will we stand at His feet in admiration, or fall to our faces in humility? Will we sing hallelujah? Or, in our overwhelmed state, will we be unable to speak? I don't know. As the song says, we can only imagine,[69] and, with our feet firmly planted on truth, imagining with anticipation on a daily basis is exactly what we should do.

If you forget everything but a microscopic portion of this entire book, remember this: No matter what we have to go through to see the Second Coming, allow your mind to be renewed to the point where you earnestly desire to see the day Christ comes to glorify Himself and fully reveal His grace. Love His appearing. Yearn for it.

This study and its closing remarks are now complete. I realize this has not been an in-depth look into all there is to say about this issue. I only desired to show you the basics, hoping it will shed a little light and make you question what we have been told, motivating you to study. I hope you have enjoyed it.

I can't begin to answer all your questions, but I would love to hear from you if this study has been a help to you. Thank you for your time and consideration of this issue.

davebussard@yahoo.com

---

[69] *Mercy Me: Almost There, I Can Only Imagine*, words and music by Bart Millard, © 1999 Simpleville Music (ASCAP), INO Records.

Recommended Reading

If you have interest in reading more about the return of Christ and feel you have exhausted your Bible study skills, here are a few books I would highly recommend reading. Although I don't agree with all the conclusions these authors have reached, each one has been a great help to me. At each of their Web sites, you will find a more in-depth summary of their work. Many of these books are also available online at places like Amazon.com.

The Rapture Question Answered: Plain and Simple, by Robert Van Kampen. Truth presented in an orderly and readable format. Everyone should check out this book. Guaranteed to make you a believer. To order, call 1-800-844-9930 or www.solagroup.org.

The Sign, by Robert Van Kampen. This book is 518 pages and is intended for the very interested person. If you want to study more than you ever thought possible, this is a must read. This is much more than just a study of the rapture, but of end-times events in general. Truth galore along with some interesting possibilities. There is also a poster-sized map included. To order, call 1-800-844-9930 or www.solagroup.org.

Before God's Wrath, The Bible's Answer to the Timing of the Rapture, Revised and Expanded Edition, by H. L. Nigro. Definitely worth your time. Gives substantial proof of the pre-wrath position while also showing many of the biblical problems with the pre-trib theory. The author is very gracious to those of the pre-tribulation theory so as not to cause dissent. To order: Strong Tower Publishing, P.O. Box 973, Milesburg, PA 16853 or www.strongtowerpublishing.com.

The Pre-Wrath Rapture of the Church, by Marvin Rosenthal. The first book I found that actually helped me understand why I kept finding nothing but holes in the pre-trib theory. Here's a man with a humble heart! To order: 1-800-447-7235 or www.zionshope.com.

The Feasts of the Lord, by Kevin Howard and Marvin Rosenthal. Not a study of the rapture but a look into the seven feasts celebrated by Israel, what they mean, how they apply to us, and their place in prophecy. Four are fulfilled and three are yet to come. Truly amazing. To order: 1-800-447-7235 or www.zionshope.com.

Revelation Unsealed, by Donald A. Salerno, Jr. Just released in 2004, *Revelation Unsealed* is the first book to approach the text of Revelation from the pre-wrath perspective. Includes many facts and ideas not discussed in other pre-wrath books, yet remains an easy read for anyone interested in the book of Revelation. A great addition to your library. To order, visit www.revelationunsealed.com.